"Just like "The Boys on the Bus" did a generation ago, [this book] gives us an intimate portrait of a major political campaign."
—Gail Sheehy, author of "Hillary's Choice"

"An entertaining, bouncy romp... an illuminating glimpse... Harpaz has written an honest book. The result is an insider's view of a female reporter grappling with a groundbreaking campaign."
—The New York Times Book Review

"Hilarious, knowing and lively."   —The Washingtonian

"Entertainingly frank."   —The Chicago Sun-Times

"Harpaz is a smart writer with a comic flair who captures the high silliness, the tedium, and the inanity of a long political campaign."
—The Buffalo News

"A charming, funny, gossipy account of life on the inside of a landmark campaign."
—Columbia Journalism Review

"Insightful, honest and funny."   —Publishers Weekly

"My dad gave me an autographed copy of [this book] when I was in high school, introducing me to a world of political reporting unlike the male-dominated one I had seen in movies and read about in other books. I felt like I was on the trail with AP journalist Beth Harpaz, and this book made me want to be a political reporter, which seemed like a far-fetched goal at the time. Today I cover the 2016 election for The Washington Post, and this book remains one of my all-time favorites."
—Jenna Johnson, Reporter

T0144718

Candidate Hillary

From Senator to
Presidential Hopeful

BY BETH J. HARPAZ

DIVERSIONBOOKS

Diversion Books
A Division of Diversion Publishing Corp.
443 Park Avenue South, Suite 1008
New York, New York 10016
www.DiversionBooks.com

For more information, email info@diversionbooks.com

First Diversion Books edition February 2016.
Print ISBN: 978-1-68230-516-4
eBook ISBN: 978-1-68230-410-5

Dedicated to all the journalists who put in long hours
on the campaign trail and those who serve as watchdogs
of power every day, everywhere.

U.S. Senate candidate first lady Hillary Rodham Clinton waves as she leaves the Autumnwood Senior Center after a campaign stop in Buffalo, N.Y., Oct. 13, 2000. (AP Photo/David Duprey)

INTRODUCTION

Déjà Vu (All Over Again)

It was the year 2000, former first lady Hillary Clinton was running for Senate, and my colleague Beth Harpaz was assigned by AP to cover the campaign.

Those were the days when reporters dialed up to get online, social media was nonexistent and the only things that went viral were Hillary's speeches, heard time and time again along the campaign trail.

With her book, "Candidate Hillary," Beth offers a look back into Hillary Clinton's history that feels notably familiar to those of us charged with covering her today. Over two years covering Hillary's effort to turn a controversial stint as first lady into a Senate seat, Beth follows her on grueling campaign swings, traces her struggles to connect with voters and valiantly tries to analyze the back-and-forth of a never-ending stream of political outrage.

It's a tale that's practically ripped from today's tweets as Hillary now tries to break through another political glass ceiling and become the first female president—a campaign that started with an early primary state listening tour modeled after the opening weeks of her Senate bid.

Yes, the scandals have been updated: Emails and paid speeches, not parades and pardons, are the controversies of the day. A $300 million family foundation has replaced a White House intern as her most pernicious personal baggage. And fears of terrorism—an issue that rarely came up in a pre-9/11 world—now dominate the political discussion.

And though technology has profoundly remade media and politics, so much about the experience of covering her hasn't changed. The clashes with a strategically unhelpful campaign staff. The notably female press corps endlessly scrutinized for bias. And the intense outpouring of emotion—be it love or hate—that Hillary seems to spark across the political spectrum.

"Candidate Hillary" reminds us that for all the political transformations and technological advancements, Hillary Clinton remains remarkably the same—intensely determined, constantly dissected and ever-unknowable.

—Lisa Lerer
AP National Politics Reporter, 2016, Washington D.C.

CHAPTER 1

Remixing
"The Girls In the Van"

In 2001, I wrote "The Girls in the Van" about Hillary Clinton's first campaign for U.S. Senate, which I'd covered for The Associated Press. A major theme of the book was the historic nature of what Hillary had done: She was the only first lady to ever run for office and she was the first woman to be elected to statewide office in New York.

Something was different on the media side too. Many of the reporters covering her campaign were women. I'd covered other campaigns for AP, but I'd never covered a race where women were more than a tiny fraction of the press corps.

Hillary's staff was filled with women too, which was a big difference from the boys' clubs that typically run campaigns. And so I named my book "The Girls in the Van," with a nod to a classic politics-and-media book called "The Boys on the Bus," by Timothy Crouse, which described the male world of the Nixon-McGovern campaign in 1972, where reporters, candidates and their handlers were all men.

Fast forward to 2015: POLITICO publishes a story called "The Women in the Van" with a photo of 18 women assigned to cover Hillary at a Democratic candidates' debate in Las Vegas. I'd actually noticed the preponderance of women covering her a month earlier when I'd covered her appearance on "The Tonight Show with Jimmy Fallon." As I joined other reporters watching Hillary's skits and interview with Fallon—in which he called her a "tough mother" and pulled her hair to prove that it was real, in supposed contrast to Donald Trump's—I couldn't help but note that all but two of the dozen reporters in the room were women.

The POLITICO article's tone was celebratory: Isn't it great that so many women are on what was once a man's beat? But the photo also sparked a debate about diversity, with readers and critics questioning whether it's any better to have a mostly female press corps (and nearly all-white) than it was to have a mostly male one.

Either way, the POLITICO article got me thinking about other aspects of my book that continue to resonate. Another theme of "Girls in the Van" was my personal juggling act as a working mother with two small boys. One memorably wacky moment was a chat I had with Hillary about potty-training my 2-year-old that made it onto a TV newscast. This was long before Paul Ryan set a new standard for work-life balance for dads by agreeing to be speaker of the House only if the GOP preserved his time home with his family. And when a young mother covering Hillary's presidential campaign recently confided that she was worried about the impact her time on the campaign trail would have on her baby, I could at least tell her I'd been there and that I knew how hard the juggle was, even though I couldn't tell her it was no big deal.

Some things I wrote about in "The Girls in the Van" will seem terribly dated to today's readers. The book was written just as old media was giving way to new media, when the daily deadlines of newspapers and TV broadcasts were replaced by the 24-hour cycle of cable news and the Internet. In the year 2000, we marveled that anyone could read email on a cellphone. We thought it was overkill to get a mere 12 emails a day (!!) from the campaign. We needed satellite equipment to send a photo to our offices. There was no Twitter to send someone's quote around the world in an instant. There was no YouTube to endlessly replay a candidate's faux pas. As such, the book is a snapshot in time, and offers food for thought about how much the media landscape has changed.

On the other hand, I believe my portrait of Hillary Clinton

has withstood the test of time. She started out the Senate campaign as a buttoned-up, standoffish first lady who once insisted that the press be escorted out of a fundraiser while she ate. She didn't take questions from reporters, she didn't rub shoulders with the public; the Queen of England was more accessible than Hillary Clinton. That changed as the campaign wore on, and by the end, she thought nothing of standing in the middle of Grand Central, literally allowing herself to be engulfed by fans.

But while she did eventually hold regular Q-and-As with the press, and even learned to joke with us from time to time, there was a part of her that remained closed off. It was ironic, given the Monica Lewinsky scandal, that we knew so much about her private life, yet we felt like we never really saw the real Hillary. Her perceived stiffness and lack of authenticity still dogs her today, on her second try as a presidential candidate, as she parades through one talk show after another, dancing with Ellen DeGeneres and telling Stephen Colbert about her favorite TV shows. You can almost hear the handlers backstage saying, "Maybe this will humanize her."

I even heard an echo in her current presidential campaign of the famous "Listening Tour" she held during the Senate race. The Listening Tour took her all over New York state, meeting with voters in small towns, churches and schools, rarely making news but often thrilling the locals. She was a famous first lady, but she wasn't taking anyone's votes for granted; she was going out and earning them. When I saw that she'd launched her 2016 presidential campaign with a series of meetings with voters around Iowa, saying, "I'm hitting the road to earn your vote," I wrote a story about how much that sounded like the Listening Tour of 1999. Or, as Lee Miringoff, director of the Marist Institute for Public Opinion put it, her presidential campaign "took out the old playbook and dusted it off."

And just as her Senate campaign started off rocky, with campaign gaffes and skeptical voters, so did her second try for the Democratic presidential nomination. Eventually, in the New York race, she seemed to hit her stride, and after a good showing in the first Democratic presidential debate, some observers wondered if she was on her way up in that race too. Maggie Haberman, who covered the Senate campaign for the New York Post and now covers Hillary's presidential campaign for The New York Times, said as much in a piece entitled, "Hillary Clinton Seeks to Recapture Spirit of 2000 Campaign." "Laden with baggage and prone to self-inflicted wounds, she needs a long runway," Haberman wrote.

In the years since I wrote "The Girls in the Van," I've heard from a lot of readers, and one of the things I'm most proud of is how many of them said the book vindicated their view of Hillary, whether they love her or hate her. Hillary supporters walk away from the book telling anecdotes about how smart she is or how tough she was in the face of personal attacks. People who hate her walk away repeating the stories that demonstrate the cynical manipulations of contemporary campaigns. So when people ask me if this is a pro- or anti-Hillary book, I reply that it's a Rorschach test. All I did was chronicle what happened when this very famous first lady ran for Senate in a state where she never lived. Sometimes that makes Hillary—and the media—look good and sometimes it makes her and the press corps look bad. The impression readers end up with depends a lot on their original point of view.

Some readers have asked me what I think of her years in the U.S. Senate. Prominent Republicans like John McCain and Trent Lott warned that she was so accustomed to being a celebrity that she would have problems assuming the low profile of a freshman senator. But she was careful, initially, to stay out of the spotlight—so much so that some of her supporters fretted that she'd dropped off the front page and into obscurity after being elected. I don't believe this was accidental. She purposely avoided making headlines in her early years as senator. Yet, in her characteristically overachieving mode, Hillary introduced 70 pieces of legislation during her first year in the Senate, more than any other novice senator and even more than a few of the senior lawmakers. Not all of her proposals made it through the legislative process, but most of the bills were either part of her agenda to improve health care and education, which helped elect her, or were related to the Sept. 11, 2001 attacks, or both.

Above all, the Senate was a good match for her nerdiness. She showed up at every briefing having done so much homework on the issues that she occasionally engendered the resentment of her colleagues. The smartest girl in the class is rarely the most popular.

How about her time as secretary of state? Sen. Harry Reid, a Democrat from Nevada, told POLITICO that "nearly every foreign policy victory of President Obama's second term" had Hillary's "fingerprints," from normalizing relations with Cuba to preventing Iran from obtaining nuclear weapons. But probably most Americans know more about two big black marks on her time at the State Department than any of her accomplishments: the 2012 attack on the U.S. diplomatic headquarters in Benghazi, Libya, in which the U.S. ambassador was killed, and her use of a private server at her home in Westchester to handle State Department emails. Both Benghazi and the email mess dogged the early months of her presidential campaign. But in September 2015, Rep. Kevin McCarthy, a California Republican who is the House Majority Leader, acknowledged that a prolonged investigation into what happened in Benghazi was designed to damage her viability as a presidential candidate. "Everybody thought Hillary Clinton was unbeatable, right?" he told Fox News. "But we put together a Benghazi special committee, a select committee. What are her numbers today? Her numbers are dropping."

That hurt the credibility of the investigation, and chatter about Benghazi and the emails seemed to fade in the months that followed. During an 11-hour congressional hearing on Benghazi in October 2015, Hillary remained utterly serene as her interrogators, mostly men, sparred and pontificated. She did get a question from one Republican congresswoman, Martha Roby of Alabama, who asked whether she was home alone the night after the attacks. Clinton said she was.

"The whole night?" Roby asked, prompting sustained laughter from Clinton, who responded "Yes, the whole night."

Clinton's unflappability during the October Benghazi hearing also showed that she'd learned something since the first time the committee called her to testify about the attack. In that earlier appearance, she lost her temper at the endless questions. "What difference does it make?" she angrily responded at one point, underscoring her critics' claims that she too often feels she need not be held accountable for her actions, as if she is above the fray. This sense of entitlement is a recurring theme in both her and her husband's public lives.

It's also a factor in the controversy over her routing of State Department emails through a server at her home. It took her months to apologize for the email debacle, and it sent Republicans into a frenzy over the lapse in judgment. That issue began to fade only after the Democratic debate where her rival for the 2016 presidential nomination, Vermont Sen. Bernie Sanders, said he was sick of hearing about "her damn emails."

Her triumphant performance overall at that debate, followed by the Benghazi hearing and Vice President Joe Biden's decision not to run for the Democratic nomination, couldn't have come at a better moment: Her campaign had become so lackluster and desperate-seeming by the end of the summer of 2015 that a reporter covering her asked me whether there had ever been a candidate who was so genuinely disliked by so many of her own supporters. Indeed, Hillary can often be her own worst enemy, thanks to her tin ear and sense of entitlement. Who doesn't mock her for remarks like her pronouncement that she and Bill, with their million-dollar book contracts, were "dead broke" when they left the White House. Barack Obama, in the 2008 campaign, made headlines when he said, grudgingly, that Hillary was "likable enough," the message being that she really wasn't likable at all.

But regardless of her ups and downs, and whatever happens to her going forward, the historic aspects of her career are what inspired me to write this book and what I still find most fascinating. After Hillary Clinton became the only first lady to ever run and win elective office, first ladies went back to doing pretty much what they always had. Hillary Clinton as first lady was a fashion disaster who lectured the Chinese government on female infanticide, and at her husband's invitation, she tried to singlehandedly overhaul the health care system. The health care proposal was a debacle, but it was the kind of bold effort that only she would have undertaken. The next two first ladies were much more conventional: Laura Bush championed literacy and early childhood issues; Michelle Obama became a fashion icon and took up issues like making school lunches healthier.

Hillary failed in her quest to win the Democratic nomination for president in 2008, but that campaign broke ground, too. Other women had run for president in the past, but none had mounted a candidacy as serious as this one, and none had ever gotten as close to the finish line. Before Hillary Clinton ran for president, we didn't even know if a woman could raise the kind of money necessary to become president. Now we know it's possible: She raised $229 million in 2008.

Hillary's stated desire to break the "ultimate glass ceiling" by becoming president is all the more meaningful given the underrepresentation of women in political office. Women got the right to vote in the U.S. in 1920, but nearly 100 years later, they make up barely 20 percent of Congress, with just 20 female U.S. senators out of 100, and 84 women in the House of Representatives out of 435 members. Despite that, women are becoming a more powerful voting bloc in the U.S. as time goes on. Nationally, more women than men have voted in every presidential election since 1964. While that's a trend that has the potential to favor female candidates, it wasn't enough to put Hillary over the top in 2008.

Her failure to win the Democratic nomination that year left a sense of unfulfilled destiny among some of the women who supported her, especially baby boomers who wondered if they would ever see a woman elected president in their lifetimes. And Hillary continues to remind voters of the historic nature of her quest. When she appeared on Ellen DeGeneres' show, the host remarked that she'd be one of the oldest U.S. presidents if elected.

Hillary responded that she'd be the youngest *woman* ever to hold the office. She also joked about taking a little longer for her break than her male opponents during the first Democratic candidates' debate, presumably a reference to gender differences in bathroom time.

Bathroom time became an issue in another debate held in December 2015 in New Hampshire. Hillary returned a few moments late to the podium after a commercial break because she'd gone to use the bathroom, and Donald Trump mocked her for it at a rally two days later. "I know where she went. It's disgusting, I don't want to talk about it," Trump said. "No, it's too disgusting. Don't say it, it's disgusting." These comments and others—including Trump saying she was "schlonged" by Obama in the 2008 race—were criticized as vulgar.

But criticizing Hillary with gender-based language and allusions, and bringing up her husband's philandering as a reason to oppose her, which Trump also began to do in early 2016, can have unintended consequences. Hillary has often done well with voters when they feel she's being victimized. It's a troubling and even sexist dynamic, especially for a candidate who wants to be judged for her strengths, not her weaknesses, but it's real. In the 2000 Senate race, a famous moment took place at a debate where the Republican candidate, Rick Lazio, left his podium onstage to walk toward her in what looked like a threatening manner. His candidacy at that point was already dimming; he just couldn't match her gravitas, but something about the image of this younger, taller man going after her at the debate also seemed to elicit a protective reaction among voters.

A similar dynamic played out just before the 2008 New Hampshire primary. Obama had won the Iowa caucuses, and Hillary needed to win New Hampshire to remain viable. At a routine campaign stop, a woman asked her a seemingly innocuous question: How did she do it? How did she manage to pull herself together every day? Hillary's voice broke as she responded that it wasn't easy: "Some of us put ourselves out there and do this against some difficult odds." The exchange, captured on video, once again seemed to trigger a sympathetic reaction among voters: Hillary, it seemed, was not a superwoman after all. She was human, and like everyone else, she admitted that just getting out there every day can be a struggle sometimes. She's often criticized for her aloofness and lack of authenticity, but at that moment, it seemed like the curtain had lifted. She went on to win the New Hampshire primary, even as her critics questioned whether her teary response was staged.

(New Hampshire voters didn't treat Hillary so kindly in the 2016 primary: Sanders beat her 60-38. While some pundits were already predicting doom for her presidential aspirations, it's worth pointing out that New Hampshire doesn't have a great track record of picking Democrats who make it all the way to the White House. Obama didn't win there in 2008 and Bill Clinton didn't win there in 1992. Jimmy Carter in 1976 was the last Democrat who wasn't already a sitting U.S. president to win in New Hampshire and then go on to win the general election.)

But the "Hillary Clinton as victim" narrative goes back much farther in time than the 2008 race or even the 2000 Senate race. It's rooted firmly in her husband's philandering, and there are many who believe that her entry into politics was in fact a form of marital payback. She got her own political career, the theory goes, for all the suffering she endured as the wronged wife of a president who had a sexual relationship with Monica Lewinsky, a 20-something White House intern. In late 1998, when word of her plans first emerged, the story was that if everything went right, she would take office in the U.S. Senate just as her husband was leaving the White House. And she would use that first step as a senator from New York, where neither she nor Bill Clinton had ever lived, as a building block for an eventual run for the presidency.

The irony of this narrative—that she became a presidential contender as consolation for being a wronged first lady—is rich. After all, she holds herself up as a female crusader and feminist role model. But she also put up with a cheating husband. One could fairly ask: Do they love each other, these Clintons, or are they merely accomplices in their mutual ambitions? That question was very much in the air back in 1998, when rumors of her Senate aspirations began to swirl the very same week her husband's testimony in hearings about the Lewinsky sex scandal became public.

One other aspect of the "Hillary as victim" story deserves a mention. In hindsight, Bill Clinton's two terms as president during the final years of the 20th century were remarkable as a period of peace and prosperity, especially in contrast to the turmoil of the first 15 years of the 21st century, marked as they were by terrorism, war and the Great Recession. Yet while Bill Clinton was president, the White House seemed to reel from one crisis to another, many of them revolving around the Clintons' personal circle, from the suicide of White House aide Vince Foster to the endless investigations into Whitewater, a real estate deal mired in corruption in Bill Clinton's home state of Arkansas. Even their final days in the White House were tainted by behavior that seemed to suggest the Clintons don't believe the rules apply to them: They rewarded donors with nights at the White House in the Lincoln bedroom; they received extravagant gifts for the home in New York they established to support Hillary's Senate run; and in the final hours of his presidency, Bill Clinton granted clemency to a felon, Marc Rich, whose wife was a major Democratic donor.

Hillary Clinton had famously complained as first lady of a "vast right-wing conspiracy" targeting her and her husband, and even in one 2015 candidates' debate, when asked whom she was proud to call an enemy, she answered "Republicans" (along with "Iranians"). Certainly the Clintons have been targets of the GOP, but she and Bill also provided plenty of ammunition, and have often allowed themselves to be drawn into a fight. Say what you will about Michelle and Barack Obama, but for the most part they've done an exemplary job publicly ignoring personal attacks, including racial hatred. The Clintons, in contrast, can't seem to resist the bait, and that's a dynamic many predict would follow her back to the White House if she won.

A few months ago, as the 2016 candidates began to gear up and I started to read more and more speculation about how Hillary would fare, a reader who'd contacted me about "The Girls in the Van" back in 2001 got in touch again. He'd bought the book to inspire his then-teenage daughter, Jenna Johnson, an aspiring journalist, and he'd even snail-mailed me the book back then to autograph it for her. He was writing now to tell me that she had indeed become a journalist, now covering the 2016 presidential campaign for the Washington Post. It was the kind of note that writers dream of getting, to learn that something you wrote made a difference in a reader's life.

That note also added to my desire to bring "The Girls in the Van" back for a new generation as "Candidate Hillary," this time also available as an e-book. Of course I thought hard about whether anybody would care about a campaign that took place more than 15 years ago, before iPhones, before Obama, before Hillary's first campaign for president. But because the candidate I wrote about is the most famous American woman in politics, and because issues that I wrote about—like women on the campaign trail and work-life balance—still inspire debate, and because it's worth considering how different the media are now, I think there's value in preserving some of these stories. As time went on, the 2016 campaign even seemed to echo the 2000 campaign in some ways: She was up in the polls, she was down in the polls, women loved her, women hated her, Bill's philandering was a big deal, Bill's philandering didn't matter. The headlines could have been ripped out of the Senate coverage.

This edition is a remix of the original. I've edited out some passages, and added new context to others. But some names from Hillary's first Senate race are better known now than they were then: Her original campaign manager, Bill de Blasio, is now mayor of New York City. Her top press aide, Howard Wolfson, played a key role in her 2008 campaign and went on to become a top adviser to Michael Bloomberg. But more important than a list of familiar names is the fact that the themes I wrote about 15 years ago remain relevant: the historic nature of her quest as a woman and as a former first lady; what it's like to be a working mother covering a political campaign; and Hillary's love-hate relationship with the public and the press, one day fighting accusations of entitlement and corruption, the next day a rock star who can do no wrong.

Finally, I believe the portrait I made of Hillary as she evolved from first lady to candidate remains an accurate one. "Candidate Hillary" explores the irony of the perception that Hillary never lets anyone see her true self: After all, thanks to her husband's sexual proclivities, we know more about Hillary Clinton's private life than we have a right to. And yet, as other candidates are lauded for their authenticity, she still struggles with how she's perceived and what she stands for. It was true in the 2000 race, and it's true now.

So travel back with me to Hillary's first turn as a candidate, and see all of this for yourself, as it first unfolded. Take a seat with the girls in the van, and enjoy the ride.

CHAPTER 2

Evolution from
First Lady to Candidate

The lead-up in late 1998 to the announcement that Hillary Clinton was running for U.S. Senate played out against the surreal backdrop of revelations about Bill Clinton's sexual relationship with Monica Lewinsky. This diary documents how absurd it seemed at the time: The humiliated first lady was not retreating behind closed doors to weep about the shame her husband had brought to the White House and to their marriage. Instead, she was making her own headlines, daring the press and the public to accept her as someone with her own history-making agenda. She had never been elected to anything; no first lady had ever run for office; and she had never lived in New York. And yet, we were hearing that she intended to run for U.S. Senate from New York.

It's hard from this point in time looking back to remember how unlikely this scenario seemed. But as this timeline from the fall of 1998 and early 1999 shows, many New Yorkers—myself included—were simply incredulous. Even Gloria Steinem, a Hillary supporter who more than anyone else alive in the U.S. is responsible for the modern feminist movement, wrote in her recent memoir: "I couldn't understand why Hillary wanted to go back to Washington ... Why ask for six more years with a target painted on her back? It seemed quixotic and self-punishing."

Like Steinem, I really didn't believe the first lady was going to run for Senate. And yet, she did.

• • •

Sept. 21, 1998

On a day when everyone else in the world is making jokes about cigars and "Leaves of Grass," the book of poems that Bill Clinton gave to Monica Lewinsky, I'm trapped in an alternate universe with Hillary.

I'm here as a reporter for The Associated Press, covering the first lady at a conference at New York University. I thought I'd be writing a story about her sniffling and sighing and pushing back the skin on her cuticles on the day that the rest of America was watching her husband's testimony about his relationship with "that woman," a White House intern half his age.

But Hillary doesn't seem distressed in the slightest. She looks serious, she's nodding, she's actually paying attention while some professor pontificates about banking and investment.

Still it seems surreal: I'm in a room at NYU with her, the victim-wife, and a bunch of academics contemplating democracy and the global economic crisis. She makes a speech describing "what makes life worthwhile: family, religion, spiritual life, free association." Meanwhile, Bill Clinton, in grand jury testimony from August that's being shown today for the first time on TV, describes his "inappropriate intimate contact" in the Oval Office with Lewinsky.

Hillary gets a standing ovation and then shakes hands, signs autographs and allows herself to be admired. Isn't she strong, they say, hushed and respectful. Isn't she poised, isn't she dignified. She's like a widow, a lioness, a doormat, and an Amazon all rolled into one. Will she weep? Or roar? Or ever stop pretending?

And now the president arrives. Everywhere else he is the laughingstock, but in this room, he's presidential. Prime ministers from England and Italy and Bulgaria are here, big men discussing big things while Hillary sits silently in the front row, a first lady listening. The president thanks her for arranging this conference; she has no reaction. She did not use his name in her speech, but he is not embarrassed to use hers. He speaks about taxation, investment and problems with the Asian banking system; everyone takes notes.

He says "the treatment of young girls in certain cultures" is "the most perverse manifestation of gender inequality"; no one titters. Hillary knows how weird this is, but she's not ashamed. Let them whisper in pity and wonder. She will not hide.

When it's over, Hillary greets the Italian prime minister but ignores Bill. Their aides escort them out like strangers. They do not look at each other or speak or touch.

I want to shout, "Can't you see this isn't normal?"

Nov. 6, 1998

A political bombshell has just dropped: New York's senior U.S. senator, Daniel Patrick Moynihan, a Democrat, has announced that he will retire when his fourth term ends in 2000. Speculation immediately begins as to who will run to replace him. Robert F. Kennedy Jr., a lawyer, environmental activist and the assassinated senator's son? Andrew Cuomo, who at the time is serving as President Clinton's secretary of housing, and who will one day become New York's governor? Carl McCall, the state comptroller? Or Nita Lowey, a likable Westchester congresswoman? On the Republican side, there's New York City Mayor Rudolph Giuliani, or maybe Gov. George Pataki.

A few pundits are crazy enough to throw out Hillary Clinton's name. A couple of people, including Charlie Rangel, the raspy-voiced Harlem congressman, tell the first lady she ought to consider it. "I thought it was an off-the-wall idea," she later recalled in Newsweek.

Jan. 3, 1999

Sen. Robert Torricelli of New Jersey, who, as chairman of the Democratic Senatorial Campaign Committee, is responsible for scouting out potential Democratic Senate candidates, says on "Meet the Press" that he believes Hillary Clinton will run for Moynihan's seat. Before Torricelli's prediction, the other Democrats have bowed out, all except Nita Lowey, who's cheerfully insisting that it's fine with her if Hillary wants to run, but reminding everyone that she's available in case the first lady doesn't work out.

Jan. 11, 1999

Chuck Schumer has already been sworn in, in Washington, as New York's new junior senator, having defeated the Republican incumbent Al D'Amato. But the ceremony is being re-enacted today in Manhattan for his New York supporters, and Vice President Al Gore is in the house. But no one really cares about what Gore has to say. Or what Chuck has to say. Instead, in the balcony where the press corps sits, we're all buzzing about someone who isn't even in the room: Hillary.

Adam Nagourney of The New York Times had a story over the weekend quoting various Democrats speculating on whether Hillary would make a bid for Moynihan's seat. "Mr. Rangel said that Mrs. Clinton, in a conversation the other day, said nothing to dissuade him from advancing her candidacy," Adam wrote. He then quoted Rangel as saying, "Me being an optimist, I consider that very favorable."

Me being a realist, I don't believe Hillary has any intention of running for Senate. It looks and sounds like an ego-boosting distraction from her husband's scandal: He's now being threatened with impeachment. Why would she want to get into a fight that she might not win after all the fighting she's been through? Why would she want to spend the last two years of her husband's term on the campaign trail in New York after expending so much effort to stay in the White House? And why would she want to be one lousy voice in 100 as a senator when she could run a university, make millions at a corporation or command audiences with heads of state around the globe on behalf of all her pet causes? The world is her oyster; New York is a snakepit. I'm convinced she's too smart to come here.

Still, I can't help but think back to that seminar at NYU. They really loved her. And she knew it. And all that applause, without anybody mentioning Monica Lewinsky, must have sounded pretty good to the world's most publicly humiliated wife.

Jan. 12, 1999

Today Bill Bradley establishes his presidential campaign fund. Al Gore formed his on Jan. 1. I can understand how a guy who wants to be president needs this much lead time, but the Hillary-Clinton-for-Senate conversation is now at full volume, too, well ahead of any other Senate race and 22 months before the election. It doesn't make sense for anybody to spend two years running for Senate.

Jan. 26, 1999

A Marist poll shows Hillary leading Giuliani 53-42 in a hypothetical Senate race.

Feb. 2, 1999

Bill Clinton attends a fundraiser for New York Democrats in Manhattan. "It's highly likely," he tells the audience, "that I will increasingly be known as the person who comes with Hillary to New York."

Feb. 12, 1999

The Senate votes today on impeaching the president, and Hillary holds a four-hour meeting in the White House about running for the Senate with Harold Ickes, a former White House deputy chief of staff who helped mastermind both of Bill Clinton's presidential campaigns.

Feb. 16, 1999

The first lady issues a statement: "I will give careful thought to a potential candidacy in order to reach a decision later this year."

Feb. 21, 1999

Hillary has just been featured on the covers of Time and Newsweek, a first lady on the verge of making history, and today Giuliani is making the rounds of the Sunday political talk shows with appearances on CNN, ABC and WCBS-TV, a lame-duck mayor itching for a fight.

"There'd probably be more of an inclination to do it if she were to decide to run," he says. Since I covered New York's last Senate race, the Schumer-D'Amato campaign, I've been assigned to cover whatever happens in this one, and I duly put together a Rudy-Hillary story. But we are still 21 months away from an election, and I still can't believe she'll do it.

April 19, 1999

Now Hillary is showing up in New York every five minutes, pretending she's just doing her normal rounds as first lady even though she hasn't spent this much time here in the previous six years. Today she attends eight events around the city in 14 hours. There's a ceremony in Central Park, a meeting about Kosovar refugees, a fundraiser for a congressman and a speech on education at Columbia Teachers College that ranks as one of the most boring events I have ever attended ("I dare you to find a sound bite," I whisper to the local cable TV news producer sitting in front of me). Hillary makes herself available for one, and only one, brief interaction with the press, and when she's asked about the Senate, she says the magic words: "I'm obviously still considering, and exploring, and am very interested. But right now I'm very focused on the situation in Kosovo."

Yeah, right.

She also talks about how much she's always liked New York and its diversity, from big cities to "rural areas that provide some of the crops you might be surprised are actually grown right here." Well, maybe she's surprised that apples come from upstate, but as for the rest of us, it's old hat, Hil. Later, she presents an award to Katie Couric at a Manhattan luncheon for women in broadcasting. Katie teases her about apartment hunting.

Meryl Streep tells a story about whitewater rafting. "The other whitewater," she giggles. And Nora Ephron makes a crack about the very un-New York wardrobe of a first lady: "You can run. You can live here. And you will never have to wear a turquoise jacket again."

April 20, 1999

Ickes introduces Hillary at a forum on something or other at Hofstra University on Long Island, and she makes a long, boring speech. But there's one bit that stands out, and it even makes a pretty good lead. She talks about the health care reform effort that the president assigned to her, the one that was a total disaster, the one that consisted of thousands of proposed regulations hatched in secret by a first lady that nobody elected and then presented to Congress like a fait accompli only to be thrown back in her face by angry lawmakers and a scornful public. And what does she say about all that today? "I'm not going to try that again, rest assured," she says in a humble, self-deprecating tone. "I come from the school of smaller steps now."

Earlier in the day she visited an elementary school on Long Island, in Syosset. Told that Eleanor Roosevelt had once been there, she says, "I'm used to following Mrs. Roosevelt. I don't know that I've been anywhere in the world, literally, that she hasn't been first."

Tonight, there's a gala dinner for the United Jewish Appeal. Giuliani has already pledged to make Hillary's statement from the previous year, supporting a Palestinian state, an issue in the campaign, and tonight she makes the first of many efforts over the next 19 months to backtrack. It was May 6, 1998, when she'd told a youth conference on peace in the Middle East that "it will be in the long-term interests of the Middle East for Palestine to be a state." Some liberal Jews here and in Israel might agree with that, but no American politician could ever get away with saying it. Bill Clinton's position has always been that Palestinian statehood is something the Palestinians and the Israelis need to work out for themselves, and tonight Hillary Clinton repeatedly expresses opposition to any "unilateral moves" in the peace process. An outsider would have no idea what she was talking about, but the 700 guests at this dinner applaud, knowing that what she's really saying is that the Palestinians better not unilaterally declare an independent state for the West Bank and the Gaza Strip.

April 29, 1999

Hillary's back in New York for the fourth time in two weeks, and I'm already tired of being forced to show up at every event 90 minutes before she does so the Secret Service agents and their dogs can search me and everything I own. I have even learned the terminology for this practice: lockdown, as in the "lockdown time is 7 a.m.," which means we, the lowly press corps, have to be present and accounted for by then—even if Her Majesty doesn't waltz in until 8:30 a.m.—or else we won't get in the door. I'm also starting to tire of events that have no news and of following her around for days without ever getting to ask her a question. Even the public's admiration for the wronged wife has cooled. The latest polls show she and the mayor are in a dead heat for a Senate race that's more than a year and a half away and that neither of them will commit to.

Today's shlep involves taking the A train, nearly to the end of the line, to a Queens junior high school in South Ozone Park where the first lady is playing principal for a day. We are ushered into the school office; the photographers complain because there's not enough room to set up their equipment. Besides, they bitch, she always walks past without turning her head. No Q-and-A either, the print reporters gripe. The whole thing sucks.

"Heads up!" someone calls as she walks into the narrow room. We are all crowded behind the counter like students clamoring for a schedule change, jostling to see her, pens poised for a quote we don't expect to get, cameras following her just in case.

Suddenly everything is in slow motion. She's pausing. She turns our way.

She looks at us. She smiles. The cameras whirr and snap. She's posing for us!

"Good morning!" she says cheerily. "How are you all today?"

She's talking to us! I am stunned. For the first time since she started making these trips, Hillary Clinton has recognized the media's existence.

And now another shocker. We'd been told that when she went into a library to talk to 30 kids in an eighth-grade social studies class, we'd have to leave the building. But now they're telling us that we are welcome to come along. We follow her through hallways decorated with handmade signs that say "The first lady is cool!" and "Happiness is a visit from Mrs. Clinton!" And then her aides, mostly White House staffers, tell us to pull up a chair, leave our tape recorders on and sit there for an hour while she chats with the students.

Right off the bat, a student has a question for her: What does she think about the bombing of Kosovo? Damn, I think to myself. Why didn't I plant a question with one of these kids about the Senate race? It hadn't occurred to me that they'd have the nerve to actually ask her something newsworthy, but this kid who asked about Kosovo, this kid's clearly on the path to a career in journalism.

"I support the continuation of the bombing," she replied. "I believe it will eventually work. I believe it is a way of punishing the Milosevic regime."

The rest of the session feels like a local-access TV show about what New York City teenagers are really thinking, except that the moderator, instead of being a school counselor, just happens to be the first lady. "I really hope we'll have a chance for me to know if there are things you want me to talk to the principal about, or even to talk to my husband, the president, about," she says in a tell-me-your-troubles-and-I'll-take-care-of-it tone of voice. "We need ideas from young people to provide better conditions for all of you."

The kids include immigrants from around the world: Trinidad, India, Puerto Rico and Guyana, and she expresses fascination that the school offers a bilingual class for students whose native language is Punjabi. Then she asks the kids about gangs and a boy mentions that the Bloods and the Lost Boys hang out in front of local grocery stores.

"Most people want to belong to a group," she responds. "They want to be part of something. How do we do a better job of giving kids good gangs to hang out in or more chances to be part of something positive!"

There's talk of the Columbine school shooting, of metal detectors and violence in video games, and a wistful admission from Hil: "I think it's much harder being a young person today than when I was growing up."

We're all scribbling furiously, checking our tapes to make sure they don't run out during this hourlong exchange, even though everybody knows that most of this stuff will never get into print. And while we can't ask questions, we can watch and listen, and that seems like a lot, considering that we thought we'd be out on the street. Something has happened here, and it's not about being principal for a day. I can't get out of my head how charming she was in the principal's office, the way she acknowledged our existence. All of a sudden, Hillary Clinton wants the media. Hillary Clinton needs the media. Hillary Clinton smiled at the media, spoke to the media.

For the first time, I think it might be true, what everyone has been saying since January. Maybe she really will run for the Senate. If she's decided she needs to have a relationship with us, there must be a reason.

May 23, 1999

Rick Lazio, a Republican congressman from Long Island, says on ABC's "This Week" that Hillary Clinton needs "an exploratory committee to find Elmira." Two weeks later, the first lady makes a point of saying she'd "been to Elmira." When the Star-Gazette newspaper, located, of course, in Elmira, runs an article questioning her veracity, her Washington spokeswoman, Marsha Berry, explains that Hillary had been through Elmira as a child on a family trip between Chicago and Scranton. That is not an obvious route when you look at a map, but maybe the attractions of Elmira were deemed worthy of a side trip by the Rodham family.

June 2, 1999

I am sitting in the hot sun on a balcony overlooking the Harlem campus of City College. Below me, 3,000 graduating students and their families are awaiting the start of their commencement ceremony. Suddenly a cheer goes up, then a ripple of applause turns into a roar, then the students rise and begin to point and crane their necks to see the person they've been waiting for: Hillary. I look down from my vantage point and fix my eyes on her. She's easy to spot, a small, blond white woman in a purple graduation gown, making her way down a path through a sea of black and brown faces at this mostly minority public university. As she walks from the plaza entrance to the stage, the students wave and reach out to touch her.

And then, spontaneously, the chants begin: "Run, Hillary, run! Run, Hillary, run! Run, Hillary, run!" At first she ignores the adulation, shrinks back from the extended arms; I can see that she's surprised by this, a little overwhelmed, doesn't know how to react. But as she continues along the block-long path to the podium, she starts looking at the students who are calling her name.

She nods hello, returns a smile, looks relaxed. One woman has written "It takes a village" on the inside of her mortarboard; she holds up the cap and catches the first lady's eye. Now Hillary's pausing to shake the outstretched hands and even stops to allow a large man to wrap her in a hug while her Secret Service agents hover nervously. By the time she gets to the stage, the aloof first lady who arrived on campus a few minutes before has all but disappeared, and in her place another woman has emerged, a woman who's running for office. When she finally speaks, she says nothing that is all that important, but her tone of voice is totally different from anything I've heard from her before. All of a sudden, there's a roar in her words, a cadence that invites applause, a rise and fall designed to rev up an audience that's already treating her, as Bob Hardt at the New York Post will write, like a rock star. Gabe Pressman, a veteran political reporter for WNBC-TV, put it this way: "We've just seen the evolution of a candidate."

Two hours later, we are at Tavern on the Green, waiting for her to speak, and the old Hillary Clinton is back. We are ushered into an adjacent room, ostensibly to interview the Democratic Party chairmen for Westchester and Rockland counties. But when we try to go back into the luncheon, we are told the area is off-limits until Her Majesty finishes eating. It seems the first lady does not want her picture taken while she dines.

June 10, 1999

In late May, on "60 Minutes II," Dan Rather asked her which baseball team she'd root for if she moved to New York. "The politic answer," she said, "since I do plan to live in New York, no matter what I wind up doing, is, I'll root for both."

Fifteen days later, she's asked the same question on ABC's "Good Morning America." "The fact is," she says, "I've always been a Yankees fan."

CHAPTER 3

The Magical Listening Tour

Hillary Clinton launched her 2016 presidential campaign with a series of sit-downs around Iowa where locals chatted about issues large and small. She did a lot of listening and nodding, and the press was allowed to observe but was not always allowed to ask questions. News was rarely made. These events took me right back to the middle of Hillary's first Senate campaign and her Listening Tour. The Listening Tour brought Hillary all over New York to meet informally with locals. It was designed to foster a humble image of her putting in the time and doing the hard work required to familiarize herself with local issues and earn voters' respect and to counteract the notion that she'd waltzed into a state where she'd never lived to have the Senate nomination handed to her by her husband's party. The events were billed as unscripted, grassroots sessions, but in fact they turned out to be tightly controlled with invited guest lists and little media access. And initially, voters were less than impressed: July 1999 polls showed her slipping behind Rudy Giuliani, the New York City mayor who was thought at the time to be her likely opponent in the Senate race. Here's what it felt like to be part of Hillary's magical Listening Tour that summer and fall, including that unforgettable moment (which I'm not exactly proud of looking back) when I asked Hillary how she felt about plastic surgery, and my ruminations on her hairdo.

• • •

I was riding in a car with a photographer for the AP in September 1999, pulling into a parking lot in Great Neck, on Long Island, for one of Hillary's Listening Tour events, when I spotted a familiar figure gesticulating angrily to a Secret Service agent posted at the entrance. It was my mother-in-law, Leah, and needless to say, I didn't expect her to be there.

The photographer readied his press pass to show to the agent, who walked toward us as we slowed down. I slunk down slightly in my seat, but it was no use.

Eagle-eyed Leah, who was about 5 feet tall and old enough to legitimately say that Eleanor Roosevelt was her favorite first lady, spotted me in the passenger seat.

"That's my daughter-in-law!" I heard her announce to the agent in a commanding tone of voice. "She works for The Associated Press!" She peered into the car and explained that she was trying to get into the event at a senior center in her hometown where she had taught an exercise class for the elderly for many years. But Leah's name was not on the list of invited guests, and even the center's director, whom she'd known for a long time, told her there's no way she could get in. So, she wanted to know, could she just come in with me?

"I can't do that," I said in a small voice, noticing that she was wearing one of her nicest dresses, with jewelry, makeup and everything, the way she did for important family gatherings and the High Holidays.

"Why not?" she asked. "Why can't I just come in with you?"

It was so simple from her point of view, but so incredibly complicated from mine. The photographer, meanwhile, was sighing and tapping on the steering wheel, impatient to get inside the building so he could grab a good spot for taking pictures and set up his gear. I told Leah I'd come back in a minute after we parked. We drove nearer to the building and got out. The photographer took his tripod and cameras inside, while I headed back to the edge of the grounds where Leah was still making a fuss.

"There you are!" she said as I approached, then took my arm, puffed herself up and introduced me to the agent in her most imperious manner.

"This is my daughter-in-law, Beth Harpaz, who works for The Associated Press. She's been covering Hillary for months now."

Then she turned to me and lowered her voice. "You can't just take me in with you?"

I explained that my name was already on whatever list the campaign was maintaining for the press, that my Social Security number was on file with the police department, and that even with all that, I still had to have my bag searched for explosives and sniffed by German shepherds every time I went inside a building where Hillary was speaking.

"For the general public, these things are invitation only," I added. "They're very strictly controlled."

Now Leah was indignant. "I know that. I tried all day to get in there. I've been on the staff of this senior center for years. I called everyone I know here and none of them would help me, not one. They said the list was made up a long time ago and there was no room to add anyone else. I'm never speaking to any of them again. Everyone on the board of directors got invited, and because I'm not on the board, I can't get in. It's ridiculous!"

I tried nodding sympathetically the way Hillary does when she's listening to people whom she can't really help, but it didn't seem to calm Leah down. Instead she became increasingly agitated and the Secret Service agent began to look a little alarmed. Sometimes they passed around Polaroid photos of people who made a fuss like this and I definitely didn't want Leah to get on that list.

"Look, you're upset, and you have every right to be," I said in my most reassuring voice, while trying to make eye contact with the agent to let him know that even though she was a little upset, this woman, a widow and grandmother of six who was old enough to be Hillary's mother, was completely harmless.

"It's just awful that nobody could get you inside, but it's not necessarily the senior center's fault," I tried to explain. "These guest lists are written in stone."

She listed for me all the people she'd spoken to that day to try to get in, everyone from the staff of the center to a couple of Hillary's local financial and political supporters whom she knew. "Nobody could help," she said, suddenly sounding exhausted.

I looked at my watch. It was almost lockdown time, the time after which reporters would not be allowed inside. I leaned over, touched her arm and looked her right in the eye. "You have to calm down. I feel terrible about this, but there's nothing anyone can do."

She shook me off and stiffened her back. "Never mind," she sniffed. "It's a bunch of phony baloney, that's all. This whole Listening Tour is phony baloney. Hillary is phony baloney. I'm going to tell everyone I know what happened here today, and I'm certainly not going to vote for her."

I sighed. "I gotta go." I gave her a hug, catching the agent's eye again to make sure he could handle this without resorting to some tactic that we'd all regret later, and was relieved to see him smile slightly and nod. He understood, and it was going to be OK.

I hurried inside. The event, like a lot of these Listening Tour meetings, turned out to be less an opportunity for the public to tell Hillary what was on their minds than a way for Hillary to make known her support for a standard Clinton administration position— in this case, a proposal to use part of the projected federal budget surplus to shore up Medicare and add a prescription drug benefit.

When it was over, she had the most intimate "avail" (journalist jargon meaning an "availability" for the press corps) that she'd ever held with us. At most Listening Tour events, there was no avail, or if she took a few questions from the press, they had to be shouted from the rear of the venue where we were always seated, over the heads of the hundred or so civilians in the audience, with several dozen of us fighting at once for her attention. Inevitably, the people in the audience would turn around and regard us with a mixture of curiosity and horror.

But this avail, in contrast, was peaceful and well-organized. We were in a small, quiet room, "pencils" (print reporters) seated in a circle in front, so that our heads didn't get in the way of the TV cameras, and "stills" (newspaper photographers) standing behind. It was mid-September and I wondered if maybe after spending the summer being followed around by us, she had finally gotten used to us and was signaling her comfort by coming closer, physically, to us than she ever had before.

We'd all been buzzing about a recent article in Esquire that was a meditation on Hillary's sex appeal, as well as another item in the New York Post that claimed she'd been having plastic surgery consultations in Manhattan. A couple of my male colleagues were arguing over who ought to ask her whether the report was true. "I'll do it," I volunteered, immediately feeling slightly guilty about my eagerness to pose a somewhat sexist question, while at the same time feeling obliged, as the wire service reporter who has to make sure the basics are covered for news outlets that might not be present, to get the plastic surgery question cleared up. We needed her on the record about it.

Personally, she struck me as a woman with very little personal vanity. She'd been mocked for changing her hairstyle, with her critics suggesting that a woman who changed the way her hair looked as often as she did couldn't be trusted. But I got the sense that she just didn't care that much. And while Michelle Obama loved the attention her bold wardrobe elicited, Hillary's choice in apparel seemed to be more about trying to come up with the right uniform for the job, without really caring much one way or the other. She wore a ball gown for the cover of Vogue, pink when she testified before the grand jury, a skirt for church, bright colors in Arkansas and upstate New York, and a black (or navy or gray or beige) pantsuit paired with a jewel-tone blouse when she was in Manhattan. The dark pantsuit with a long jacket became a virtual symbol of her campaign, and eventually couturier Oscar de la Renta was revealed to have been the designer behind it. It became such a classic staple of her wardrobe that a museum exhibition of de la Renta's work even included one of Hillary's pantsuits along with the fabulous evening gowns he designed for red carpets. Hillary's pantsuits also had staying power, becoming her go-to outfit more or less for the rest of her career. In her Twitter biography, she even called herself a "pantsuit aficionado."

Another change in her personal appearance during the Senate campaign that became a go-to look was her new hairdo. Never again would we see the headband and the shoulder-length tresses. Instead, she had a short, simple, blond helmet with a wave on one side that could be pouffed up or sculpted for a more dramatic look. It was businesslike yet sophisticated, up to date without being faddish, and age-appropriate but not at all dowdy. It was the hairstyle of a corporate lawyer or a busy editor or a Wall Street executive, the hairstyle of a smart, self-assured, influential woman, channeling all the right messages for a woman seeking elective office. It also permanently replaced the ever-changing coiffures that had set her apart from so many of the previous, more staid first ladies and led her critics to ask whether her positions on the issues might be just as changeable as her hair.

Of course I felt guilty about sharing the public's and the media's fascination with her appearance. But I often justified it in my head by reminding myself that when I'd interviewed Sen. Chuck Schumer for a profile, I'd asked him where he bought his suits. (The answer was Gorsart's, a downtown discount place.) It seemed to me that you could tell something about people by how they looked: Were they vain or oblivious to appearances, thrifty or extravagant, old-fashioned or on the cutting edge? Later, when her opponent Rick Lazio entered the race, the press devoted almost as much space to discussing his appearance (his grin, his boyishness, the little wavy lock of hair over his forehead) as they had devoted to hers. (One afternoon on the Hillary van, we even debated whether the flecks of gray in Lazio's hair were natural, caused by the stresses of the campaign, or purposely dyed in to suggest maturity. Someone finally called a relative who worked as a hairdresser, who assured us, after hearing a detailed description of the gray, that it sounded perfectly natural.)

In the 2016 campaign, plenty of time was devoted to the weirdness of Donald Trump's hair. And Marco Rubio's boots, which added a couple of inches to his 5-foot-10 height, had a moment of fame too. "Have they lost their minds?" Rubio asked when he found out that a photo of the boots had gone viral. Bernie Sanders scolded a New York Times reporter for asking him whether he thought it was fair that Hillary's hair was getting more attention than his. "I don't mean to be rude here," Sanders told the reporter. "I am running for president of the United States on serious issues, OK? Do you have serious questions? ... We have millions of people who are struggling to keep their heads above water, who want to know what candidates can do to improve their lives, and the media will very often spend more time worrying about their hair than the fact that we're the only major country on earth that doesn't guarantee health care to all people."

But fortunately, Hillary was more patient with me the day I had to get comment on the plastic surgery report. I signaled that I had a question for her after a couple of other reporters had asked theirs, and she nodded my way. I mentioned the Esquire and Post reports, but then tried to camouflage the crass "was she going for plastic surgery" question by asking whether she viewed the media's interest in her appearance as sexist.

To my surprise, rather than expressing annoyance, she leaned her head back and laughed long and hard. It started out like a giggle but ended up almost giddy, like a belly laugh. It was a laugh I'd hear again and again during the campaign when she was asked a potentially embarrassing question; I later realized that it gave her a few seconds to formulate a response, usually one that sidestepped the question, and also suggested that despite the sensitive nature of whatever she was being asked, she had nothing to hide.

But this was my first exposure to the laugh, and I was impressed that she appeared so carefree about this subject. We all waited, pens poised, tape recorders running, until she finally stopped laughing, and then started scribbling while she spoke. "I have never talked to anybody about plastic surgery," she said unequivocally. When she'd heard about the Post report, she said, "at first I just laughed about it. But I want to set anybody's mind at rest who has any concern about this." She neatly avoided making a judgment as to whether such reports are sexist, saying instead that she hoped coverage of her campaign would focus on "what we just heard from the senior citizens ... public education, health care, jobs, campaign finance reform or gun violence."

I left the building when the avail was over to find the Secret Service guy standing alone at the parking lot entrance. My mother-in-law had given up and gone home.

A few days later, at another event, I saw Howard Wolfson, communications director for Hillary's campaign. I told him about my mother-in-law's demand that I take her into the event, thinking he'd find it amusing, or that he might even get defensive about how tight the Listening Tour guest lists were.

He did neither. Instead he just said, "Why didn't you just ask me? I would have gotten her in."

"What?" I said, somewhat flabbergasted. "Are you kidding? I'm not supposed to ask a campaign staffer to do a favor for my mother-in-law."

He shrugged. "I've done it for other people," he said nonchalantly.

"You have?"

He nodded and walked away.

For a minute I felt terrible. I probably could have gotten Leah in and saved her all that angst, but it had never even occurred to me to try.

Then my Righteous Journalist's Conscience kicked in: Wouldn't it be a conflict of interest to ask Howard to do you a favor like that? It was different from asking him to help out with something that made it easier to write a story.

On the other hand, the entire incident was also a perfect illustration of why the Listening Tour was so often described in news accounts as "much-ridiculed." Leah was right; in some ways, the Listening Tour was phony baloney. These were not the open town meetings that we had been led to expect, the type of forum that might be publicized a few days in advance with tickets made available to the community on a first-come, first-serve basis. Instead, these were high-security, invitation-only, carefully formatted programs.

True, the campaign did not handpick the guests, but whatever local organization had been asked to host the meeting did handpick them. As a result, most of the audiences were friendly to the point of worshipful; typically people would get up and tell sad stories about not having health insurance, or inspiring stories about making the transition from welfare to work, or complicated stories about some local controversy, and Hillary would chirp, "I appreciate your raising that issue! It's something I care deeply about!" Afterward, she'd be mobbed by admirers, many of them carrying just-bought copies of her book "It Takes a Village" for her to sign.

Each Listening Tour event had a theme: gun violence, education, health care. But especially in the beginning, the press often did not get to ask any questions, and the news value had more to do with the sheer novelty of a first lady sitting around some dingy auditorium in an out-of-the-way place chatting with a bunch of locals than the actual content of anything she said. (The reporters who covered these events did, however, get very good at nodding their heads the way Hillary did when she was listening. Here's how: Without ever blinking your eyes, you bring your chin way up, so that your neck is painfully extended, then you slowly drop it way down to your chest, then you move your head an inch to the left or the right and repeat. To make it even more authentic, say, "You know, that's an excellent point. Thank you for bringing that up.")

The idea for the Listening Tour was born in the second week of April 1999 in a memo from Mark Penn, who became the campaign pollster and one of Hillary's chief advisers. Penn had just done his very first poll for the first lady's potential campaign, and in the memo to her, he outlined how receptive he'd found upstaters to be to the idea of her candidacy, and how large that group of potential votes was. He also coined the phrase "Listening Tour" to describe how he thought she should introduce herself to a state where she had never lived: as an unpretentious visitor stopping by the neighborhood to meet people and learn what was on their minds.

At the same time, Mandy Grunwald, the campaign's media consultant and a former aide to Moynihan, was separately suggesting a virtually identical approach: It was imperative for Hillary to visit all 62 counties, and to engage in a preliminary get-to-know-you stage before formally declaring herself a candidate.

But the focus on upstate was not uncontroversial within the campaign. "What the hell is she doing in Delaware County? Why isn't she at Zabar's?" is how one campaign source summed up the anti-Listening Tour sentiment. Harold Ickes, who'd been the first lady's premier confidant as she weighed the idea of running while the impeachment drama played out, was perhaps the most skeptical about trolling for votes north of Westchester. "He thought we were spending too much time upstate and that we should be spending more time in the suburbs, where we had the biggest problems," the source recalled. "But if you looked at the numbers carefully, she had more potential, more to gain, upstate."

The pro-Listening Tour contingent eventually came to include Hillary. "She could feel by the kinds of questions people were asking that it was the right thing to do," the source said. "And every time the downstate press ridiculed the Listening Tour, we basically laughed, because we knew that upstate it was tremendously important." But several campaign staffers acknowledged that it wasn't just the press. As one person put it: "There were people in the campaign making fun of it, too."

Another staff member pointed out that sometimes upstaters even came to Hillary's defense if the press started asking questions that had nothing to do with local issues. Shortly after Hillary was quoted in Talk, a short-lived new magazine, blaming Bill's philandering on his childhood, the first lady held a Listening Tour event at a furniture factory upstate in Jamestown.

Reporters were all over her, trying to get her to elaborate on what she'd said in Talk, "and finally a woman in the audience got up and basically said, 'Someone is finally here listening to us. You guys shouldn't be asking those stupid questions!'" the staff member recalled.

The staffer added that "just the concept of her going to these places got people excited. These were areas that have largely been ignored," both by the political establishment of the state and by the economic boom of the 1990s, "and now the first lady of the United States was coming here and listening to their issues."

But wasn't it true that Hillary intended all along to go through with her candidacy, and that the Listening Tour was never about testing the waters? "That's not unfair to say," another adviser said, "but we didn't want the full campaign to start right away. The point of the Listening Tour was to not be seen as presumptuous, but for her to go and earn it."

As for the media's biggest criticism, that the Listening Tour events were overly controlled, rather than being open, town-meeting-type events, campaign staffers insisted that for the most part, the Secret Service dictated what was and wasn't allowed in the beginning. "We were in uncharted territory for letting a first lady do the kinds of things that she was doing," an aide said. "To do a completely general public meeting, that wasn't possible. They wouldn't have let us." But some of the controls, the aide admitted, were "because of her comfort level also."

Despite the invitation-only guest lists, sometimes a hostile questioner would somehow get into the audience. At the first Listening Tour event I covered, an education event in Westchester in mid-July, the guest list included teenagers who were active in student government, local educators, PTA moms and women who'd been stars in a welfare-to-work program. Then one woman with three kids got up and said that because the first lady is "a Democrat who needs to raise funds, the teachers union is very important." She went on to suggest that, as a result, Hillary wouldn't be willing to buck the unions on issues like kicking out unqualified teachers with tenure. "But as a parent, I know there are some teachers I hope my children will not get," she added.

Hillary, who did, in fact, court and win strong support from teachers unions, smartly sidestepped the fundraising crack and instead said something about how she believed schools should "invest more authority in the principal in terms of hiring and retention of teachers."

Afterward, the mother of three was mobbed by reporters desperate for someone to say something other than "Hillary really was listening! She was so friendly! She's such an inspiration!" The woman admitted that she was a Republican who planned to vote for Giuliani and added that Hillary "doesn't even live here. She never has lived here." When we asked Howard to comment, he just smiled and said it proved that, contrary to everyone's perceptions, the campaign was not controlling the guest lists.

The press corps was then escorted to vans that were waiting to take us to Jones Beach on Long Island, where the first lady planned to have lunch in a restaurant and take a leisurely, impromptu stroll along the shore, or as leisurely and impromptu as a first lady can take when she's trailed by camera crews, print reporters, Secret Service agents, her press aides and her personal assistants.

We spent the ride from Westchester to the beach trying to make sense out of some of the comments Hillary had made at the forum, such as expressing support for making college tuition tax-deductible. It was a strange way for a would-be candidate to make her positions known, throwing out tidbits during Listening Tour events such as this Westchester forum on education, without elaborating or giving us any opportunity to pin down the details. How much money was involved in this tax proposal? Who would be eligible for the deduction? Was this the same proposal Schumer already had on the table? No one, including her fledgling staff, some of whom were in the van with us, as they would always be throughout the race, seemed to know, and without a Q-and-A or a press release—the basics that any normal campaign would provide—it was difficult to write about the proposal coherently. A normal candidate would just hold a press conference on the issue and then answer questions about it, but I got the feeling that her handlers thought it would be too shocking, somehow, for a first lady, a carpetbagger and a neophyte candidate, to simply lay out where she stood, all at once, in a straightforward fashion. Instead, we were being exposed to her opinions one tiny bit at a time, in a roundabout way, as if these positions were organically arising during the Listening Tour programs we were attending instead of being carefully formulated beforehand.

(Interestingly, college tuition breaks came back as a theme in Hillary's 2016 campaign, in her proposals to lower interest rates on college loans, cap loan payments at 10 percent of income, forgive some debts after 20 years and make tuition free at community colleges. Republicans said the proposals would raise taxes, but other Democrats also have proposals to decrease college costs.)

Despite all our griping about the Listening Tour, it was sort of fun being part of Hillary's Excellent Adventure. The campaign had printed up laminated press passes, in full color, bearing a map of Westchester and Long Island and the words "Hillary Rodham Clinton, U.S. Senate Exploratory Committee Listening Tour." As they dangled from chains around our necks where we carried our regular photo IDs, which were issued by the police department, these special credentials served two purposes. One, they made it easier for Hillary's staff to recognize who was part of her pack; and two, they made us feel really cool. You often came across people who kept White House passes or "Trip of the President" credentials in full view long after they ceased to need them, and having one of these Listening Tour passes on your chain when the Listening Tour was front-page news conferred a similar status. It was like being part of the "in" crowd in high school. Sure, we made fun of the Listening Tour; it was touchy-feely in an Oprah-esque way, but there was also something oddly groovy about it, about the very words Listening Tour, that brought to mind the roadies' bus for a rock 'n' roll show instead of a press van.

The New York Observer captured it perfectly with the caption "Magical Listening Tour" on a cartoon of Hillary singing an altered line from "I Am the Walrus." "I am she as you are she as you are me and we are all together."

When we got to Jones Beach, a crowd had already begun to gather, having heard on local newscasts that Hillary was headed to the boardwalk.

They burst into applause when she finally appeared, and within minutes she was surrounded by several hundred people jostling to be near enough for a handshake or a greeting. While the Secret Service hovered, she posed for pictures with shirtless men and bikini-clad women. Then she looked out at the sparkling water and blue skies and confessed, like the carpetbagger that she was, that she'd never been to Jones Beach before.

"I've heard about it literally all my life," she said, smiling a dazzling smile, her big eyes as blue as the sky, "from many friends who would come here and spend lots of glorious summer days. I'm just delighted to be here."

But none of the beachgoers seemed to care that this woman who'd never lived in New York and never been to this beach before was thinking about running for office here. The press might get bogged down in petty particulars like that, but these people were simply too starstruck to care.

"I shook her hand!" gushed a beach maintenance worker as he walked away from his encounter with Her. Another woman dreamily told me, "She touched my shoulder!"

Clearly, Hillary wasn't just any old candidate looking for votes; she was a world-class celebrity whose magic touch nearly rivaled the pope's, and these were her adoring fans.

It had been only a week earlier, on July 7, 1999, at a press conference with Sen. Moynihan on his farm in upstate Pindars Corners, that Hillary had announced the Listening Tour. Moynihan's wife, Liz, had told the first lady early on, "Whatever you do, don't announce in the ballroom of the Sheraton Hotel on Seventh Avenue in Manhattan like every other candidate!" So instead of the hotel, the campaign was launched on Moynihan's farm, where the senator walked with Hillary down a dirt road toward the scores of waiting reporters, mumbled something about "Plutarch's Lives" and "Pilgrim's Progress," and then declared, "I think she's going to win." (Two months later, when he endorsed Bill Bradley for president, he said, "There's nothing the matter with Gore. But he can't be elected." Say what you will about Moynihan; he knew how to pick 'em.)

Hillary then announced that she was about to embark on the

Listening Tour, traveling around the state to learn about New Yorkers' concerns. A day earlier, she had officially formed an Exploratory Committee for the U.S. Senate, a legal entity that enabled her to raise money in anticipation of a likely campaign.

Then came her first real questions from the press. Wasn't she a carpetbagger? "What I'm for is maybe as important, if not more important, than where I'm from." What about all the scandals? "New Yorkers will make their own judgments about that. I think we've moved beyond all of it."

And finally, this one: "A lot of people see you as the No. 1 victim of the Monica Lewinsky scandal. I wonder if you see yourself as a victim and if you think you benefit from the sympathy vote?"

Her answer sounded like a response to a different question. "I'm looking forward to meeting with New Yorkers, and I think they'll have a lot to tell me about what they think about me and the positions that I have."

She spent several days "listening" upstate, then embarked on the suburban phase of the tour. The day after the stroll on Jones Beach, she presided over a discussion about gun violence in Rockville Centre, on Long Island. Her co-host was U.S. Rep. Carolyn McCarthy, a former nurse who had entered politics as a gun control advocate after her husband was killed and her son injured by a gunman on the Long Island Rail Road in 1993.

Also present was Alice McEnaney, whose son, Jason, had been shot in the groin when he disarmed a gunman holding 36 people hostage in a classroom at the State University of New York at Albany. It was a story familiar to most New Yorkers because it was one of the nation's first school shootings, and because of the dramatic heroics involved in ending it.

"On Dec. 14, 1994, we got a phone call that's every parent's nightmare," McEnaney told the first lady. "My son was involved in a hostage-taking at SUNY-Albany. He disarmed a gunman. He had been shot in the process."

"You've really spent a lot of time in the years since your son's murder —" Hillary started to say, only to have McEnaney interrupt, saying: "He wasn't murdered. My son's alive!"

"Thank God," Hillary responded.

Jason, in fact, was in the audience of about 60 people, seated in the first row.

The reporters in the back of the room were astounded by the screw-up. Had Hillary's staff failed to brief her properly, by not telling her that this young man would be in the audience and that he had survived a school shooting, or had she become confused? We looked at each other incredulously.

When the session was over, I called my office. I was torn about whether to lead with her blunder. On the one hand, it seemed a little unfair to make such a big deal out of the type of mistake that anybody could have made. On the other hand, it was just about the only unscripted moment in an otherwise canned event. If that wasn't the lead, what was? The first lady supports gun control? We knew that already, and therefore, by definition, that was not the news. It also highlighted the fact that she was new to the state: If she'd been living here, she would have known the story about the school shooting. And it raised questions about her campaign's competence. Why hadn't they briefed her?

The verdict back from my editors was to lead with it, and to find out whether Hillary had met Jason beforehand or been told that he had survived.

Our Q-and-A had been brief and chaotic, one of those situations where people were shouting questions from the back of the room. It hadn't occurred to me to try to confront her about the mistake, and nobody else had either. Howard wasn't traveling with us that day, but the other campaign staff members on hand said he was the only person who could comment on the mix-up. Another reporter on the van, hearing that AP was planning to lead with the flub, flatly said, "We're not leading with that," giving me pause once again about my own approach. And when I finally reached Howard by cellphone, he was peeved. After all, his job was to spin the news in the most flattering way toward his candidate. "This shouldn't be the lead of your story," he said, and asked who at the AP he could appeal to. I deferred to my bureau chief, Sam Boyle, and Howard called him directly to try to talk him out of it.

But it remained in the lead of our story, and Howard, for his part, refused to say whether Hillary had been told before the forum that Jason had survived or that he was in the room. "Mrs. Clinton was sharing her concern for the mother of a gunshot victim and misspoke" was all I could get out of him. "That's it."

The same day, a new poll registered the voters' initial reactions to the Listening Tour and the first week of Hillary's exploratory campaign:

Giuliani was now leading her by a half-dozen points. Both the Post and the News had front-page headlines the next day announcing Hillary's "slip is showing," and it seemed that the novelty of following Hillary around on her don't-call-it-a-campaign-trail was already wearing off.

Now we were recording the deflating reality of a novice candidate making no news for us on a good day for her, and bad news for her on a good day for us. The free ride from a worshipful public and a respectful press only lasted as long as she gave a flawless performance, and just a week into her Listening Tour, that phase had already ended.

CHAPTER 4

You People in the Media

How does this rank as an example of the juggle faced by working moms?
It's the night before Thanksgiving and I'm standing on the front steps of my
building, hoping my kids don't get hit by a car running after a soccer ball, as I
conduct a phone interview with Hillary's ex-boyfriend to see if he'll say whether
she smoked pot. He wouldn't give me a straight answer, but he did give me a
lecture, one that I'm familiar with, having heard it from many others. It starts
out, "You people in the media," and regardless of the person's political leanings,
it basically blames the media for emphasizing all the wrong things about every
candidate ever.

Here's hoping that if you've read this far in this book, you don't believe the
media is responsible for everything that's wrong with politics. As a journalist for
AP, quite honestly, all I ever wanted to do was get the facts straight and try to
tell both sides of the story. But then, as now—with fact-checkers in the 2016
race debunking claims by Donald Trump about mass celebrations in Jersey City
following 9/11—just making sense of what's being said in a campaign is not
always easy.

• • •

It was around 9 p.m. the night before Thanksgiving in 1999. I was
standing on the front steps of my apartment building in Brooklyn,
shouting into my cordless phone. It was cold and windy and dark, and
I was talking to a guy named David Rupert, who dated Hillary when
she was in college. He'd been interviewed in a new book, "Hillary's
Choice," by Gail Sheehy, and in an excerpt that was released before

the book came out, he'd hinted that Hillary might have smoked pot. Hinted it by saying she hung out one weekend in 1969 with a crowd in which "some of us were inhaling," but refusing to actually come out and say she partook. "I don't have to go there but you can read between the lines," he'd told Sheehy. So one of my editors called me at home to see if I could track down the guy and get him to clarify.

I'd actually called his house a few weeks earlier when a different excerpt from the book had turned up in Parade magazine. I'd found that excerpt more compelling; in it he'd said they eventually broke up because he wasn't ambitious enough for her. "I never stated a burning desire to be president of the United States," he told Sheehy. "I believe that was a need for her in a partner."

I remembered the name of the town where he lived and was able to get the number again with no trouble. I spoke to his wife both times and left messages, but while he didn't call me back the first time, tonight, for some reason, he has. So now I have a pencil in one hand, my reporter's notebook in the other, and my left shoulder hunched up to keep the phone from falling. And I am trying to pin him down, one way or another, as to whether he actually ever saw Hillary smoke pot.

"Look, it was very, very kind of you to return my call," I say in my most urgent yet polite yet assertive yet ingratiating tone of voice, the tone I reserve for people like this, people who don't know me from a hole in the wall, people who, for some ungodly reason, agree to speak to me when, if they had any sense at all, they'd be slamming a door in my face or hanging up.

"But I just really need you to answer this one question, and then I won't take up any more of your time: Did you ever see Hillary smoke pot? I just need a yes or no answer, and then we'll be off the phone."

I glance up as I talk to make sure my kids haven't gotten run over chasing their ball in the street. There they are, two little blond blurs darting around the parked cars in front of the building, a streetlamp illuminating their game.

"No, no, you can't do that!" the big one, Danny, yells to his younger brother, Nathaniel, as the little guy bends over to pick up the ball. "No hands! You idiot! How many times do I have to tell you? In soccer there are no hands!" Danny runs over and kicks the ball away from Nathaniel's grasp, back toward his own turf. Nathaniel looks up at me, a tearful pout forming on his round little face as he stands in the pool of light from the lamppost.

I was pretending, in this phone interview, to be a normal, hardworking journalist, the type of person who would make a call late the night before Thanksgiving from an office or a car or wherever someone like that would be. If I'd tried to make the call from inside the apartment, the kids would have blown my cover in an instant, screaming for this or that and me with no way to tune them out. So I brought them out on the front steps hoping that they would entertain themselves for just a few minutes without pestering me while I did my job. But now, with Danny yelling at Nathaniel and Nathaniel about to cry, it looked as if I were going to have to intervene anyway and reveal my true identity as a mother tethered to two small children and their incessant demands.

"Maaaameeeee!" the little one screamed, then let out a wail.

I gave Danny my angriest look, the one where I make my eyes really big and scrunch my lips up, then put one hand over the mouthpiece of the phone and stage-whispered, "Stop it now" while wagging the forefinger of my other hand in their direction. Then I turned my back on them and, facing the wood-and-glass front door of the building, tried to resume my conversation.

"You still there?" I said, stepping back into my urgent-sounding yet sincere reporter's mode. "Sorry about that." We'd been going around in circles for a few minutes now, me restating the question every way I could think of, and him not giving me a straight answer no matter what I said.

"Yes" came the reply in a tone both wearied and annoyed. "I'm still here. But you're not going to get me to say what you want me to say. If Hillary wants to tell you people in the media, or the voters, whether she did or did not smoke pot 30 years ago, or whenever it was, that is entirely up to her."

I stopped myself from saying, "Then why did you bother calling me back?" But there's no need to, because he immediately launched into the explanation himself in the form of a "you people in the media" lecture.

The one about how we shouldn't be chasing after all these scandals, we should just be sticking to the issues. The one that leaves out the part about how readers are a lot more interested in the scandals than they ever are in the issues. This conversation was going nowhere fast. I stuck my pencil in the wire coil of the notebook and turned back to face the kids. Somehow Danny had managed to get the game going again. He was kicking the ball toward Nathaniel and Nathaniel was following it with his eyes, then chasing after it, then pouncing on it.

"No hands!" screamed Danny. He looked up, saw that he had my attention, and whined, "Mom, he won't play by the rules!"

Nathaniel's eyebrows started to crinkle again. "Maaaaameeeee!" The cry echoed off the buildings across the street. I heard a window go up; someone undoubtedly was about to call child welfare to turn me in.

Danny heard the window, too, and was now grinning with delight at having caused Nathaniel to disturb the neighbors. And Nathaniel was picking up the ball, holding it above his head, and throwing it with all his might into the street, grunting slightly with the force of his toss.

I covered the mouthpiece of the phone again, called out, "Don't run into the street," and dashed down the steps to the curb. I put myself in the space between the two cars parked in front of the building to bar any potential recovery of the ball by the children, and turned my attention back to the phone, figuring there was no point in wasting this guy's time or my own any longer. If he was going to divulge anything about Hillary smoking pot, he would have already done it by now. Time to wrap things up.

"Right, well, again, I appreciate your calling me back," I said abruptly. "Have a good Thanksgiving, sir, and thanks very much for your time."

I put the phone down on the hood of the car next to me. I looked up the street, saw no oncoming traffic, ran across to fetch the ball from the other side where it was stuck under a car, and gave it a one-handed toss back to Danny, who smiled proudly as he caught it on the fly.

The boys resumed the game and I called the editor in Washington who'd asked me to track this guy down. I read her his quotes and she agreed that they weren't strong enough to put on the wire. There was no point in running a story that raises the question "Did she smoke pot?" if we can't answer it. I'd also already gotten a call back from Howard Wolfson, one of those "I can't believe The Associated Press would stoop so low as to consider running a story like this" calls. Howard also said that Hillary had already denied ever having smoked pot, so I passed that on to the editor, too. The new Sheehy book was to be delivered to me at my in-laws' house in Massachusetts the day after Thanksgiving, so I told the editor I'd read it as soon as I got it and call her then.

I was just about to bring the kids inside with me when I saw one of my neighbors coming down the street. He's a lawyer who used to be a newspaper reporter, and I guess he'd been working late and was just now arriving home. He has two boys like me, but his wife doesn't work, and his kids certainly weren't outside playing soccer in the dark the night before Thanksgiving.

"Hi, there. What's going on?" he asked casually as he gets to our stoop.

"Oh," I said, feeling ridiculous all of a sudden, "I'm just… just calling Hillary's ex-boyfriend to see if she ever smoked pot."

He knew I was covering Hillary, so it wasn't completely absurd, just mostly absurd. I briefly explained about the Sheehy book, and how I'd happened to have the ex-boyfriend's phone number, and how it's just one of those calls that has to be made right then and there, so I'd brought the kids out and…

He looked slightly amused, and maybe also slightly relieved that he'd given up journalism. We said goodnight and went inside.

My husband was working late, as he often did. It was the only way we could manage our schedules. He worked late because he did the morning routine with the kids: waking up, breakfast, dressing them and getting them to school and day care. I started work at 8 a.m. and was supposed to leave at 4 p.m. for the end-of-day routine: picking up the kids, making dinner, supervising Danny's homework and doing Nathaniel's bath. I liked to say that when my day at the office was over, my real job began.

Of course, once I started covering Hillary, leaving at 4 became a thing of the past. It was highly ironic to me and several other mothers in the press corps that a candidate who talked so much about the importance of family life, of supporting working parents, of the juggling that women do between their careers and their kids, would actually cause us to spend less time with our children than we used to. One day Hillary showed up more than an hour late for a visit to an emergency day care center in midtown that serves working parents when their normal child care arrangements fall through. Because this first event ran late, so did the next one, and I ended up being late to pick up my children that day. "Why are you so late?" the big one whined when he saw me as I forked over the $5 late fee to his after-school program.

Only Hillary could highlight the child care crisis in America while simultaneously causing a child care crisis in my life.

Even my Thanksgiving holiday ended up revolving around Hillary.

Sheehy's book "Hillary's Choice" was delivered to my in-laws' house early Friday morning, and I spent the day reading it and writing up a story about it. One of the most fascinating tidbits in the book was a quote from Harold Ickes, who'd become her top campaign adviser, telling Sheehy: "This is a race for redemption. It's really that simple." After her failed health care reform effort, Whitewater, Lewinsky and the impeachment scandal, winning a Senate race "would permit her supporters to say there was a lot more here than anybody thought: 'You guys were wrong!'" Sheehy quoted Ickes as saying.

The timing of the book's publication was perfect. The

Clintons had just closed three weeks earlier on a $1.7 million home with two fireplaces and a swimming pool in Chappaqua, in suburban Westchester.

Of course, like many of the Clintons' financial ventures, this one was immediately criticized as unsavory. The first couple had allowed Democratic Party fundraiser Terry McAuliffe to put up $1.35 million of his own money as collateral for a mortgage. The deal was so widely criticized that Hillary and Bill finally went out and got their own conventional loan from a regular mortgage company. (McAuliffe went on to serve as chairman of the Democratic National Committee and as chairman of Hillary's 2008 campaign before becoming governor of Virginia in 2014.)

Then, three days before "Hillary's Choice" was released to the press, Hillary ended speculation that she was about to drop out of the Senate race. At the time, her poll numbers were flagging and she was trying to recover from a series of high-profile mistakes, including opposing clemency for a group of Puerto Rican nationalists without consulting anyone from New York's large Puerto Rican constituency, and kissing Palestinian leader Yasser Arafat's wife during a visit to the Middle East. Clinton friend-turned-foe Dick Morris and other columnists and critics were loudly predicting that she was on the verge of quitting. But during her first press conference back in New York after the trip to Israel where she and Suha had kissed, Hillary allowed an ardent supporter, teachers union chief Randi Weingarten, to ask, "So, is it yes, or is it no?"

Everybody's cameras and tape recorders were going and we were practically salivating, pens poised, ready to take down her response and get it back to our offices by cellphone. "The answer is yes!" Hillary responded, beaming like a woman who's just gotten engaged. "I intend to run!"

Since we'd already been covering what looked and felt like a campaign for months, this seemed a little anti-climactic. But it did unleash a fresh round of profiles and front-page stories about the novelty and history of a first lady running for office. Endorsements and money started to flow in from unions and Hollywood types, a trend that would continue till the end of her $30 million fundraising effort. One noteworthy name turned up early and often among Hillary's big-money donors: Walter Kaye. Kaye, who had made a fortune in the insurance business, was a frequent and generous donor to many Democratic Party causes and also happened to be friends with Monica Lewinsky's mother. That had led Kaye to recommend Lewinsky for the White House internship. But Hillary was happy to accept his support for her Senate campaign; he and his wife ultimately donated more than $100,000 to the state Democratic Party to be used on Hillary's behalf.

The "I intend to run!" event also led to another go-round on the Sunday morning political TV talk shows by her campaign staff and her detractors. My favorite quote from the Sunday shows was from Ickes, when he was asked on CNN about the "race for redemption" statement in Sheehy's book that suggested Hillary was being handed a Senate run as a consolation prize for the Lewinsky affair.

"I don't recall it," Ickes said matter-of-factly. "I remember Gail calling me and asking me if I would interview for the book. And I told her I would not. I may have had a conversation with her on the phone. I don't recall the quote."

Two months later, I had my own interview with Ickes (and I'm hoping that if anybody asks him about it as a result of this book, he doesn't decide to say that it never happened). I'd called him a few times but never gotten a message back, and I really wanted to interview him for a profile I was writing of Hillary. Since it was impossible to get a sit-down interview with her, even though Howard had been promising one to the AP for months, I figured Ickes was the next best thing. One day I noticed, on the AP Daybook, which was a daily calendar of newsworthy events sent out to all the local media, a listing for a reception in honor of the labor law firm where Ickes worked, Meyer Suozzi English & Klein. I decided to go and see if I could corner him. Only one other reporter was there, Bob Hardt from the New York Post. Although I'd seen Ickes on TV, I wasn't sure what he looked like.

Bob, who knew Ickes, pointed him out and asked if we could

chat. A little while later, Ickes escorted us into a back room, shut the door, and proceeded to pontificate, at our invitation, on why Hillary was running for Senate.

"She has had a very long career of public service," he told us. "Most people don't understand that. Most people look at Hillary through the prism of that of first lady, and all that that has entailed: Whitewater, impeachment, etc. The fact is, if you go back and look at her history, you have a young woman who was very committed to public service."

He added: "Hillary looked around and started thinking about the alternatives. She's not driven by making money. I don't think she wanted to go around just making speeches. Or writing books. She really wanted to continue her devotion to public service. People kept saying, 'The world is your oyster.' She could do this, she could do this, she could do this. There are many things she could have done. But she also understands how short the half-life of a first lady is. The half-life of a first lady is pretty damned short. And the more this society becomes focused on celebrity, the shorter the half-lives of formers become."

I asked him about the Sheehy quote she attributed to him—that this was a race for redemption.

"I do not see this as a race for redemption," he said emphatically. "You don't undertake something this difficult—you're running in one of the most complex states in the union—against a potential opponent who has some very strong credentials, a very tough race, you don't do that to redeem yourself. You don't go through the agony of coming in, establishing yourself, raising money that it's going to take to run this race, for redemption. You do it because you have a very profound sense that you want to continue a career in public service. Some people have said, 'Why do you want to be in the Senate?' Being in the Senate ain't chopped liver! A lot of people want to be in the Senate. You don't work miracles in the Senate, but if you're in it for the long term, you can do a lot…. As she looked over the range of alternatives, this was the alternative she chose."

He went on: "She also understands that this is not going to be given to her. She's going to have to work for the trust of the people of New York. There was initially all this talk about the first lady. A lot of people came out to see her just because she was the first lady. There was a celebrity factor. That has worn off now. Everybody understands, first and foremost, Hillary, that she has to work for this, that she has to earn the trust of New Yorkers. If you look at the issues, she is on the right side of a very broad range of issues. But there is the question that haunts many people: Why is she doing this? And who is she?"

I have heard a lot of Hillary's supporters attempt to explain why she ever bothered to go to all the trouble of moving to New York, facing down the carpetbagger taunts, subjecting herself to grillings by the New York media on all the Clinton scandals after spending the previous six years doing the same thing in Washington. And I have heard Hillary's opponents explain that she stayed with Bill out of sheer ambition, and that the Senate seat in New York was nothing more than another step by another power-hungry Clinton to regain the White House in a shower of personal glory. I've even heard Hillary, on numerous occasions, defensively contend that she always wanted to live in New York, and that she sees the Senate as the best way to keep working for the causes that are important to her. Of course, it's easy for us in the media to be cynical about all of that, and I'm not saying I will ever abandon the view that raw ambition and some kind of marital payback played a role in Hillary's decision to run for the Senate. But until I heard Ickes explain it his way, I don't think I fully understood what it was all about.

I later realized that Ickes was party to a battle over the direction Hillary's campaign was taking; other campaign staffers told me that he wanted to spend more time cultivating the suburban vote and thought the Listening Tour and extensive efforts upstate would not pay off the way they did. Ickes' political orientation was also slightly to the left of where the campaign was usually headed, and even on internal debates such as how to win over Jewish voters, he wanted an emphasis on traditional liberal social issues instead of having her concentrate on shoring up her credibility on Israel. In the end, it appeared that Ickes had lost many of those battles to other voices in the campaign, and the election results, with Hillary's success upstate, may have proved the others right. But there was no denying that his ability to explain why she was doing it, what motivated her and what she wanted to accomplish was better than anyone else's. As far as I was concerned, he had explained it even better than Hillary could.

After spending most of Thanksgiving at my in-laws' house obsessing over "Hillary's Choice," I tried to explain to my sister-in-law why reporters found Hillary so annoying. She wouldn't answer questions like a normal candidate, I said. She held this silly Listening Tour, she made all these mistakes, she was involved in all these scandals, she'd never lived in New York, she'd never held elective office...

So what, said my sister-in-law, who grew up in New York. A lot of New Yorkers agree with her positions on the big issues. They don't care about all that other stuff. They just want someone to go to the Senate who'll represent their points of view. It's like Ted Kennedy, she said.

Ted Kennedy! I nearly shouted. What about Chappaquiddick? Some people think he oughta be in jail!

Actually, even if he'd been convicted, it would only have been for criminally negligent homicide, and he'd certainly be out by now, my husband calmly interjected. (Both he and my sister-in-law are lawyers, and I frequently feel at a professional disadvantage in arguments with either of them, since I am trained to see both sides, and they are trained to prove that the other side is wrong.)

But my sister-in-law had a bigger point to make, and that was that the people of Massachusetts, where she'd lived for more than 20 years, keep re-electing Ted Kennedy because he fought for all the liberal values they supported. He might have been the whipping boy of the right-wing pundits, but his constituents loved him. That, my sister-in-law added, was something "you people in the media" didn't understand.

It was my second "you people in the media" lecture in a week. I was starting to hate those people in the media myself.

CHAPTER 5

I Didn't Mean
to Play Gotcha

For a city of 8 million people, sometimes New York feels like a small town. You've heard of six degrees of separation? I think it's more like two here. Maybe that explains why the man who was Hillary's 2000 campaign manager, Bill de Blasio, was connected to me in so many different ways. He bought a house in my Brooklyn neighborhood from my husband's college roommates. He sent his daughter to the day care center where I sent my kids. My younger son played on basketball and baseball teams with his son Dante, who later made a famous campaign video supporting de Blasio's bid for mayor, and his daughter ended up in the same high school as my older son.

And here's why I'm mentioning all of this. When my older son needed a speaker for a fundraiser at the school he attended with de Blasio's daughter, I suggested he ask his classmate if her dad would oblige. At the time, de Blasio was the city's public advocate, a kind of ombudsman position, and not only did de Blasio oblige by showing up and giving a great speech, but before the event began, he took my son aside and told him the story of the day I caught Hillary's campaign unprepared.

I was stunned that he even remembered, but I always wondered whether he'd gotten any flack from Hillary for the incident he recounted. As the Senate campaign wore on, he seemed to be less and less in her inner circle, and years later, she did not endorse him for mayor until he had already won the Democratic nomination. (One of his opponents for the mayoral nomination was Anthony Weiner, husband of Hillary's righthand woman at the State Department, Huma Abedin. Weiner was a congressman at one point, but he had been forced to leave Congress amid a sexting scandal that eventually ended his mayoral ambitions as well.)

Perhaps as payback for Hillary's late mayoral endorsement, de Blasio famously held back his endorsement of Hillary for president for months, saying he wanted to see her take more progressive positions. When he finally did endorse her, her campaign put his name low on a long list of other less prominent individuals supporting her 2016 campaign.

Who knows what the bad blood was really about, but certainly the story you're about to read—the one de Blasio told my son—shows that her 2000 campaign team, which was at least nominally being run by de Blasio, was not preparing her on local issues as well as it should have.

. . .

It was early December in 1999. I arrived at O'Neill's Restaurant on Third Avenue at exactly 9:30 a.m., just as Hillary's schedule said. But the Secret Service guy posted at the entrance was someone I'd never seen before. "Sorry, you're too late," he said brusquely when I took out my press pass.

"Too late? It's 9:30," I said, looking at my watch.

"You were supposed to be here before 9:30."

I tried the old "Listen, I'm with The Associated Press. If I'm not in there to cover this, I'll get in trouble, but you'll be in even more trouble, because the only way every newspaper in New York state gets this story is if I'm inside."

It didn't work. "Sorry, I can't let you in. We already swept everybody's equipment," he said, referring to the search they routinely do using bomb-sniffing dogs.

"Equipment? I don't have any equipment. I don't have a camera. I don't have a tripod." I plopped myself right down on the floor next to his shiny black shoes, yanked open my knapsack, and started pulling out everything inside. "All I've got is a notebook, a pen, a tape recorder, and my lunch. You wanna see my lunch? Here it is." I pulled the plastic cover off the container in which I'd packed leftover beef stew from last night's supper. It wasn't a pretty sight, cold with gravy congealed on chunks of meat and potato, all emanating a very un-breakfast-like smell.

Someone once told me that when the agents give you a hard time about searching your bags, just pull out the little case where you keep your tampons and they get so flustered that they give up. I was just about to go for the Tampax when Wire Ear had a change of heart.

"Oh, you're not TV? That's all you had to say. Go ahead." He waved me up a narrow staircase to the second floor. I don't know whether it was a true epiphany on his part that one woman with a small knapsack did not constitute a camera crew, or a judgment that someone who was carrying around greasy leftovers was probably not the type to also be carrying a bomb. Either way, it got me in the door. Still, it left me whining to myself, as I often did, "Why can't this just be a normal campaign?" Other politicians were so happy to have the AP cover them that if you were running late and called ahead, they'd wait for you to arrive before they started.

As usual, the room where the press conference was being held was not nearly big enough for the dozens of reporters who'd shown up. All the seats had been taken long ago. I repeated my "Why can't this just be a normal campaign?" mantra in my head and squeezed against the wall next to Adam Nagourney from The New York Times. A few minutes later, I spotted Howard Wolfson and Bill de Blasio, who'd been named Hillary's campaign manager four days earlier. I'd known Bill for a long time because we'd served together on the board of a day care center that his daughter and my oldest son attended together. If Howard and Bill were here, Hillary was in the building. It was time to cue up my tape recorder.

The press conference started a minute later. It turned out to be one of those squishy tributes to Hillary by her adoring fans—in this case a variety of Irish-Americans, including the chairman of Friends of Sinn Fein, the publisher of Irish America magazine, a representative of the Ancient Order of Hibernians and U.S. Rep Joe Crowley, a Queens Democrat who was anti-abortion but who appeared by the adamantly pro-choice first lady's side with puzzling regularity. I heard Crowley saying that "when the history of Ireland is finally written, it is my hope the Irish people will remember the Clinton administration. The first lady has been there four times! She was the first first lady to go to Northern Ireland! And when that history is written, remember Hillary Rodham Clinton's efforts!"

Call me cynical, but I sort of doubted that Hillary Rodham Clinton would be prominently featured when the history of Ireland is finally written. And while I understood that these guys were legitimately thrilled by the Clintons' support for the Irish peace process, I didn't have a clue what I was going to do for a lead. I scrounged around in my head, playing a sort of free-association game that sometimes helps me come up with a decent angle. OK, what do New York readers know about the Irish? Well, there's the St. Patrick's Day parade. Its organizers, the Ancient Order of Hibernians, had for years refused to let a gay contingent march. The gay group had sued, but the courts had sided with the Hibernians, saying that as a Catholic fraternal group, it had the right to exclude gays. As a result, for the past 10 years, the parade had featured protesters and arrests, with some politicians marching and other more liberal officials staying away.

I heard Hillary say something about how every St. Patrick's Day, she attends a celebration at the White House. It occurred to me that this could lead to an interesting little story about the conflicts between her roles as first lady and as Senate candidate. If I could get her to say she'd be in Washington on March 17, I could then state that every other local pol would be in New York either marching, or making a point of not marching, in the parade.

The Q-and-A was a mess. As usual, there were way too many reporters who had something their station or paper needed to pin down, and there just wasn't enough time to get to everyone. Nobody ever got to ask more than one question, and there was never any opportunity to follow up.

Finally Hillary looked in my direction and I managed to make myself heard. "Are you going to march in the St. Patrick's Day parade?" I called out.

She paused as if she'd never thought about this before, then broke into a broad smile. "I would hope so!" she cooed.

I was flabbergasted. A liberal Democrat like Hillary Clinton couldn't possibly intend to march in the St. Patrick's Day parade! How could she not know about the gay controversy?

She was supposed to say she'd be in Washington on St. Patrick's Day! If she wasn't going to be in Washington that day, she was supposed to demur and say she wasn't sure what her schedule would look like in March, three months from then.

Within a split second, the demeanor of the press corps tangibly changed. We went from standing around listlessly, barely paying attention, to being on high alert and scribbling like crazy, leaning forward and practically holding our breath to make sure we didn't miss a single word as she finished her response. The change was so stark that even Hillary sensed it. You could see her pausing for a minute, quickly scanning the room and the people standing around her to try to figure out what about her answer had caused everyone in the room to shift gears, almost begging for a clue about what was wrong. But with nothing else to go on, the best she could do was to hastily add to her "I would hope so!" declaration a caveat: "As long as I've got lots of good company… "

But it was too late. She'd just made news unintentionally, which is never how politicians want to do it.

Adam was smiling. "Great question," he whispered to me.

I glanced over at Bill and Howard. They both looked miserable. They realized she'd fucked up, and by extension, so had they. Bill, my former friend! Howard, who would probably never return my phone calls again! I started having a conversation in my head with myself. I hadn't meant to trap her! Honest! I didn't mean to make her look like a carpetbagger! I thought she knew!

Then I realized I wasn't supposed to be feeling bad about this. I was supposed to be feeling glorious! I was supposed to be feeling proud!

How could her staff have sent her to a press conference about Irish-Americans in New York without telling her about the controversy over the parade? If there was one thing everyone in New York, Irish or not, knew about St. Patrick's Day, it was that every year a bunch of gay protesters got arrested. The protesters usually included several gay Irish-American politicians, like State Sen. Tom Duane and City Councilwoman Christine Quinn (who was herself gay and years later would face off against de Blasio for the Democratic nomination for New York City mayor, which de Blasio won). But I realized just then that neither Duane nor Quinn was up there with Hillary. Who put together the guest list for this shindig anyway?

I started praying that somebody would please ask her a follow-up question. Maybe she did know about the gay controversy. Maybe she didn't care, which would have been ironic, because Adam had a story in the Times that day about how Hillary disagreed with the president on the "Don't ask, don't tell" policy. She'd told a group of gay supporters at a fundraiser earlier that week that she thought the policy didn't work, and that she believed gays should be allowed to serve openly in the military.

So it didn't make sense that she would now turn around and thumb her nose at the gay community on the parade. On the other hand, maybe she just felt that she couldn't say no to marching in the parade when she was surrounded by a bunch of Irishmen.

But it seemed far more likely that she didn't know about the controversy, or that if she did know, she didn't understand what a big deal it was. She'd already made Puerto Rican officials mad over a controversy involving the Puerto Rican nationalist group, the FALN, and she had spent much of September apologizing, explaining and pledging to do a lot of consulting with community leaders in the future. Then in November came the infamous kiss on her official first lady visit to the Middle East, where she'd attended an event with Palestinian leader Yasser Arafat's wife, Suha. Suha used the opportunity to accuse the Israelis of using "poison gas" against Palestinians in the West Bank, contending that the chemicals had poisoned water supplies and led to a cancer epidemic. The visit ended with the smooch between the two first ladies that showed up on the front pages back in New York.

Hillary spent the rest of her campaign explaining the Suha kiss, variously saying that, in the Middle East, a kiss is like a handshake; that she'd had a bad translation of Suha's remarks and didn't realize until much later how "offensive" they were; and that, as first lady, she couldn't very well cause an international incident by rebuking Suha to her face or refusing to kiss her goodbye.

It all seemed pretty mealy-mouthed in contrast to Mayor Rudolph Giuliani, who was her likely Republican opponent in the Senate race. Now he was a guy who loved creating international incidents. In 1995, he'd had Arafat kicked out of a concert at Lincoln Center celebrating the 50th anniversary of the United Nations, saying he didn't think terrorists ought to be enjoying the good life in New York. He also made no apologies for marching in the St. Patrick's Day parade. It wasn't that the mayor didn't support gay rights; he did and had passed one of the strongest domestic partnership laws in the country to prove it. But he also thought the Hibernians had every right to invite whom they chose to their party, and he didn't see the merit of the other side's argument.

But we didn't know whether Hillary had weighed the pros and cons of marching and reached the same conclusion, or if she was simply unaware. Nearly everybody was going to lead with her parade commitment the next day, but nobody had asked the crucial follow-up question.

Now the event was over and reporters were starting to deconstruct what had happened. One said that even if we had followed up, there would have been no way to get her to admit she'd screwed up. But somebody else pointed out that we could have said something like "Mrs. Clinton, are you aware that very few other Democrats march in this parade?" That wording made it clear there was a controversy over the parade without giving away what it was. It would have been the perfect way to test her. I wished I'd thought of that earlier, but it was too late now. If this were a normal campaign, I said to myself, we could stay here until every last question was answered. If this were a normal campaign, we could get her on the phone to clear this up or get another Q-and-A at her next event, later in the day. But this wasn't a normal campaign, and none of that would ever happen.

I walked over to Howard, who was spinning so fast he looked dizzy.

"It wasn't a firm commitment that she made," he was saying to a group of reporters standing around him scribbling madly in their notebooks. "As a general statement of principle, not everything you do is going to make every person happy. And in this particular instance, we'll get back to you with the details as to whether or not she's marching… "

Only much later did I learn from a campaign aide what had really gone on. It wasn't that she had never heard of the gay controversy, but, said the aide, "she had a frame of reference and that's all. It was not entirely news to her, but she had no sense of the intensity of it, the history, the depth."

When she said "I would hope so" in answer to the "Will you march?" question, "she was responding from a generic perspective, from a national perspective. Of course you don't want to insult them," the aide said. But at the same time, "some part of her was realizing that something was going awry and that's why she broadened the answer. She knew there was a problem. So she managed to say, basically, 'I'll march if other good, decent people march.' She was acting incredibly clever. And we were all absolute idiots for not thinking to brief her on this earlier, and in our discussions of this later with her, we duly noted that we had left her out there on this one, and she duly noted that we had left her out there. … We all kicked ourselves."

The aide added that the campaign also felt the disclosure of her opposition to "Don't ask, don't tell" had been mishandled. This was, potentially, a huge story, a way of currying favor with gay voters, and a sign that she was willing to disagree publicly with her husband's administration and influence the president's thinking on a controversial issue. Yet she had revealed her position on this issue at a private fundraiser that was closed to the media, and when someone who'd attended the fundraiser had leaked it to The New York Times, the campaign lost an important opportunity. Not only would other newspapers pay less attention to the story once it had appeared in the Times, but it would ultimately get lost in the controversy over the St. Patrick's Day story.

"We had no business doing something as important as that at a fundraiser," the aide said.

Interestingly, Hillary was rarely a leader on gay issues. She did not declare support for gay marriage, for instance, until 2013, when she finally said in a videotaped statement that "gay rights are human rights, and human rights are gay rights." It was an echo of a famous speech she'd made about women's rights nearly 20 years earlier in Beijing, when as first lady she denounced female infanticide, saying, "Human rights are women's rights and women's rights are human rights, once and for all."

The same day as the Irish news conference, Hillary attended a luncheon for a foundation headed by Denise Rich to raise money to fight leukemia, the disease that had killed Denise's daughter. I'd never heard of Denise Rich before and couldn't have imagined how important she'd become after President Clinton left office and a scandal erupted over his pardoning her ex-husband, the fugitive financier Marc Rich. Denise's name came up a few times during the Senate race as one of the Democratic Party's top donors, but no one paid much attention at the time. Even though she'd written a number of Top 40 songs, she wasn't well known to either the press or the public; her visits to the White House and her donations to the Clinton library in Arkansas wouldn't be news for more than a year to come.

Nevertheless, when her public relations person approached me at the leukemia fundraiser that day to ask if I wanted to interview her, I said, "Why not?" You never knew when someone might say something that could turn out to be significant.

I remember being impressed by Denise's elaborate makeup and her dramatic, but slightly spaced-out demeanor; she tearfully told me about her daughter's life and death, how important this annual leukemia fundraiser was and how grateful she was that Hillary had agreed to headline it this year. I was completely ignorant of how big a player she was in Democratic circles, and stupidly responded by suggesting that she have Barbara Bush speak at the fundraiser the following year because Bush's daughter Robin had died of leukemia, too, in 1953 at age 4.

Denise gave me a slightly horrified look. "Barbara Bush?" she asked, her tone of voice suggesting an unspoken "Why would I want to invite her?"

I repeated my explanation about the former first lady's daughter. Denise nodded politely and murmured something about not having known about the Bush family's connection to the disease, but the look on her face remained uncomprehending, as if what she really wanted to say was: "You don't get it. I'm an important Democrat. I don't play with GOP first ladies." Finally I gave up, thanked her for her time, and walked back to the press area of the hotel where the fundraiser was being held. It was only much later that I realized why Barbara Bush wasn't a suitable candidate to headline Denise Rich's leukemia fundraiser. My flub was almost as bad as Hillary's.

But that day, I didn't think there was anything particularly newsworthy about my or Hillary's interactions with Denise. I had the St. Pat's controversy to write about, and that was the news of the moment.

By the time I got back to the office that day, Howard had already called several times and left messages, including a statement he wanted in my story: "She plans to march, and believes all such parades and celebrations should be inclusive." Except that we all knew it wouldn't be inclusive, so what the hell did that mean? The whole thing was rapidly devolving into a bucket of spin, and I started wondering if I'd be blacklisted from now on as the reporter with the trick questions and have an even harder time than I already did getting my turn at the press conferences.

I decided to feel Howard out on the subject, and a few days later I asked him if he was pissed at me for asking the question.

"Nope," he said breezily. "It was totally fair." That was one good thing about Howard—as far as I knew, he never held a grudge.

Even when you wrote a story he thought was unfair, and he called up to complain or sent angry emails telling you what for, the next day you had a clean slate. Sometimes he was less than helpful, or unresponsive, and that often made my job difficult. But at least he wasn't vindictive and didn't take things personally. Campaigns have good days and campaigns have bad days, and the mark of a good press secretary is that he treats the media the same way on the bad days as he does on the good days.

Four months later, on March 17, after explaining 100 times to all her gay supporters that she believed their concerns were important, too, Hillary did march in the St. Patrick's Day parade. And was met with boos and cries of "Carpetbagger!" every step of the way. (Of course, half the people shouting those things were from New Jersey.)

She also marched in just about every other parade held on the streets of New York and was wildly cheered at some, such as the Puerto Rican Day parade and, yes, the Heritage of Pride parade, held to celebrate gay pride. It seems the Puerto Rican community forgave her for the FALN blunder, and the gay community forgave her for marching on St. Patrick's Day.

But the kiss with Suha Arafat was not as quickly forgotten. When she marched in the Salute to Israel parade, she was booed nearly as much as she had been on St. Patrick's Day.

All this marching on Fifth Avenue led some of my colleagues to conclude that the campaign had made a commitment early on for her to participate in all the city's major parades, and therefore, even if she had known how controversial the St. Patrick's Day event was, she would have given the same answer. Certainly she didn't want to get trapped in a liberal Democrat's box of just going for minority and urban votes. Just as she made major outreach efforts upstate, to women, to blacks, and to Jews, she didn't want to leave out the white ethnic or the white Catholic vote, and that probably meant marching on St. Patrick's Day no matter what.

But the entire incident surrounding the press conference where I asked the question (the run-in with the Secret Service agent, the difficulty in asking anything, the impossibility of posing a follow-up or getting something clarified in a straightforward fashion) left me looking back wistfully on the Schumer-D'Amato Senate race of 1998. I didn't know how good I had had it then. There was no security to go through. You could walk up and ask the candidates questions whenever you needed to. It was a normal campaign.

I was moaning about the contrast one day to Adam, who had also covered Schumer-D'Amato, and he said he thought the media access problem was a simple matter of Hillary running "a Senate campaign on the scale of a presidential campaign."

I realized he was right. The sheer number of reporters, 20 or so on a light day, 50 to 100 reporters at a big event, made it impossible for Hillary and her staff to respond adequately to our needs. You could tell just from the way phone calls were handled. At the press office for the Republican Senate candidates, first Giuliani and later Rick Lazio, the Republican congressman, phone calls were answered on the second ring and immediately turned over to someone who could actually answer your question. But I eventually gave up trying to reach the Clinton campaign through their office phone. It was always busy, and even when I got through, I almost always got trapped in a voicemail system that, as far as I could tell, was never checked for messages. When I mentioned the contrast in phone systems to Karen Dunn, who worked with Howard in Hillary's press office, she said, "What does that tell you about the other side?" Well, either they're a lot more efficient and responsive than the Clinton campaign, or more likely, they don't get nearly as many phone calls. Hillary was the news in this campaign; Lazio was merely The Other, and even Rudy was Only the Mayor.

Hillary's fame and its flip side, her security needs, also made it virtually impossible for her to do campaigning in malls and subway stations the way other politicians do. The closest she ever came was shaking hands in Grand Central, which she did three times.

Each time, within moments of her arrival, crowds of hundreds of people formed instantly, reaching halfway across the terminal's cavernous waiting room. Near the end of the campaign, she held a meeting in a Chinese restaurant in Flushing with Asian community leaders, and while she was inside, word got out in the neighborhood. By the time she emerged a half-hour later, the street outside the restaurant was jammed so tight with hundreds of people chanting "Hillary!" that it was completely impassable. Mounted police were ordered to do crowd control to keep traffic moving.

Shortly after she moved into their new home in Chappaqua, Hillary went to the local Grand Union supermarket. No reporters went along; it was apparently supposed to be a normal grocery-shopping outing. But her description of it afterward made it clear that Hillary simply can't go grocery shopping like a normal person.

"I went to the supermarket in Chappaqua ... and I could not get up and down the aisles," she told Michael Tomasky in New York magazine. " ... I can't seem to get anywhere without drawing so much attention that I can't really do what I came to do. I suppose I could go to the theater, because the lights go out. But I don't know how to do this. I'm having a really hard time." No wonder the first President Bush didn't know what a scanner was when he visited a supermarket during his administration.

And while most politicians rely on the media to help them communicate their ideas and self-images to thousands and sometimes millions of voters whom they can't possibly meet individually, Hillary was already, by the time she began campaigning, the most famous woman in the world. I almost never attended a Hillary event without running into someone who was doing a story on her for the international press, and by the time the Senate campaign was over, I'd met reporters from Brazil, England, France, Germany, Holland, Italy, Japan, Norway and Turkey.

Why did their audiences care about Hillary? "In France she is a star," Laura Haim, who worked for a French TV station, Canal Plus, told me.

"She's powerful, independent, bright, modern. She's what every French woman wants to be." Which seemed tres bizarre, since so many American women view her as exactly the type of person they don't want to be: a humiliated wife.

Every one of these foreign reporters would complain about the lack of access and about her staff's nonresponsiveness, and ask local reporters like me for tips on how they could get an interview with her. How would they get their stories done without a one-on-one, they would fret. And to every one of them I would give the same answer: "The lack of access is the story. Hang around for a few days and you'll see what I mean."

In February of 2000, when she launched her campaign for the umpteenth time, this time with Bill Clinton by her side at an event in Purchase, New York, she decided to do away with her last name. Who needs the formality of a surname when your first name is relatively unusual and your fame is unparalleled? Elvis, Cher, Madonna, Oprah and now, Hillary! Until February, Howard had always, when speaking to us about her, referred to her as "Mrs. Clinton" (although he called her Hillary in person), and her schedules and press releases always had her full name, Hillary Rodham Clinton, printed on top. (In the 2016 presidential campaign, she dropped the Rodham and went simply with Hillary Clinton, apparently no longer needing to remind voters that she was the kind of woman who still used her maiden name; ironically, she only began using her husband's last name after he lost a gubernatorial race in Arkansas and her image as a career woman was deemed to be a problem.) But the banner used as a backdrop at the Senate campaign kickoff in Purchase read, simply, "Hillary," and from then on, the campaign press releases also referred to just plain "Hillary," no last name required. Later in the year, when the presidential campaign was in full swing, there were even buttons that read "Gore-Lieberman-Hillary."

I guess "Al-Joe-Hillary" just didn't cut it, and "Gore-Lieberman-Clinton" was more than the vice president could bear.

Of course, dropping her last name was also a way of trying to make her seem less formal, less reserved, more accessible and friendly. But one of the great ironies of this transformation was that Hillary was on a first-name basis with everyone except the reporters who covered her.

She called us by our first names, but we never called her by her first name. To us, she was always "Mrs. Clinton."

I remember interviewing Schumer after he'd won the election but before he'd been sworn in. I started to call him "Senator," then interrupted myself and asked, "What is your title now? Senator-elect?" "Just call me Chuck," he replied. I couldn't imagine Hillary ever inviting us to call her by her first name; and if we had, somehow, it would have seemed disrespectful. John Riley of Newsday did it once when asking her whether she'd mischaracterized Lazio's position on privatizing Social Security. "Hillary! Hillary!" he called out forcefully to get her attention.

It worked. She looked at him, and so did the rest of us, and then she finished answering his question.

"I've always called people I cover by their first names," John told me later. "Somehow, the notion that you weren't supposed to do that with Hillary had gotten inside me, just like everyone else. But there was no rational reason for it that I could see, and it seemed to be part of an aura that caused her to get special treatment and insulated her from a certain type of scrutiny. We could throw jabs and she knew how to duck and move, but it was against the rules to get inside and work the body. It seemed absurd that she didn't get called by her first name, so I consciously decided to do it."

One of the best parts of covering a campaign is all the inside jokes the reporters have. This was a big part of "The Boys on the Bus," and it was a big part of covering Hillary, too. We memorized her speeches and mouthed them along with her, we played silly games on the van and we made up songs about her. One of my all-time favorite Hillary songs addressed this whole issue of her first name. It was a spoof of a 1995 hit called "One of Us" that asked, "What if God were one of us?" The parody went like this:

What if Hil was one of us? Could she tawk like one of us?

A verse in the original song speculated about what to call God to his face, and the matching verse for Hillary went:

If Hil was her name... would you call it to her face?

It was also odd that Hillary never appeared on any Sunday morning TV talk shows during the campaign. She didn't avoid TV entirely; she appeared several times on her friend Rosie O'Donnell's show, was interviewed by WCBS-TV reporter Marcia Kramer on a weekday afternoon show, showed up regularly on the morning talk shows like "Today" and "Good Morning America," and also did an interview for Lifetime. All of these outlets had predominantly female audiences, so they were strategic choices given her campaign's effort to cultivate support among female voters. But none of them were hardball political shows like NBC's "Meet the Press" or ABC's "This Week." On those shows Hillary would send her male surrogates— Howard Wolfson, Bill de Blasio, Harold Ickes, James Carville, Ed Koch or Charlie Rangel. Occasionally she'd send one of her female advisers, Mandy Grunwald, a former Moynihan aide and now a high-priced Washington consultant. But she never went herself. Meanwhile, both Giuliani and Lazio made a point of blitzing the Sunday morning shows.

Did Hillary and her campaign simply deem these shows an inefficient way to reach the New York voters who needed convincing? Were they afraid that more national exposure than she was already getting would do even more to mobilize the Hillary-haters around the country who were donating millions of dollars to her Republican opponents? Or were they worried that she'd blunder under questioning by big-gun interviewers like Brit Hume and Tim Russert? Once, a few weeks before Election Day, I asked her if she was ever going to do the Sunday morning TV circuit. "I'm going to be talking to the voters of New York and the press of New York," she said.

After the election, several of her campaign aides explained that they always felt the New York-based media had generally given her a fair shake, while the cable talk shows and out-of-town press focused more on the White House scandals, her personality and other issues.

"It was an interesting dichotomy," one adviser told me. "You all reported on who she was as a candidate. You would listen to what she had to say and report it." The rest of the media, the adviser felt, seemed less concerned with the substance of her remarks than her style. Even at the end of the campaign, the adviser recalled, commentators on some of the cable TV shows were still complaining that "she never talks to the press, she's the Queen of England. ... By then, there was an avail practically every day."

It was true. By the time Election Day drew near, basic media access had improved dramatically. The avails became more frequent and more orderly; Hillary became more accustomed to answering questions about whatever was in the news that day, and her comfort level with us increased to the point where she was actually friendly and funny. When I and another AP reporter had a private interview with her in Buffalo in February of 2000, we had so many questions that had never been asked of her that we could have sat there for hours. (We only got 45 minutes.) But in July, five months later, when we interviewed her in Corning, there was little new ground left to cover. Yet in the second interview, she was much more personable and at ease with us.

Shortly after the Corning interview, I ran into Jesse Drucker, who had covered the campaign for a few months for Salon. I told him about how much nicer she was being to everyone, and he said, "Yeah, but did she open up?" Well, no, I had to admit, she hadn't, and I didn't think she ever would.

I was with my sister-in-law when I ran into Jesse, and afterward she said to me, "What makes him think that Hillary should open up to him?" Well, some politicians do reveal their inner feelings, especially in New York, and you're never left wondering how they feel about anything or where they stand. But others don't. Hillary, it seemed, would always be in the latter category. It wasn't just logistics that limited her media access. It was also that the woman who had suffered more public humiliation in the White House than any other first lady in history had gotten through it by telling people that the choices she made in her marriage were her business and nobody else's.

She wasn't going to cry or scream or name-call or give out any juicy tidbits, and that applied not just to questions about her marriage but to questions about everything else, too. Some people respected her for it; others held it against her. She'd taken the Queen Elizabeth approach to dignity in the face of dirt, but that didn't always go over big in the land of Oprah and Jerry Springer.

Early on in Hillary's campaign, AP photographer Bebeto Matthews had been told by Howard that he would let us take some "behind the scenes" photos of her. We imagined an interesting photo array of Hillary in her campaign war room, meeting with her top advisers; Hillary in her van, exhausted after a long day; maybe even Hillary powdering her nose right before she gives a speech. But it never happened.

In the fall, we asked again for better photo access, and again, it never materialized.

Lazio, who eventually became Hillary's Republican opponent for Senate, provided the contrast for what might have been: his campaign allowed AP photographer Richard Drew to stick to him like glue, riding with him in his personal van and spending time on the bus with his wife, Pat, and their two daughters. The resulting photos of Daddy Rick painting his little girls' fingernails with felt-tip markers, Rick and Pat catching a quick snooze in their seats between campaign stops, Lazio gazing out the window right before Election Day, looking very much like a man about to be defeated, were widely used in newspapers around the state. Sometimes you'd catch someone on Hillary's staff staring at a photo of Lazio in the paper, as if the person couldn't figure out why that photo had been used instead of a picture of Hillary standing at a lectern. On election night, we had a photographer in Lazio's suite, but nobody saw Hillary until she came out to give her victory speech.

So guarded were Hillary's private moments that when we did manage to observe one, it was unforgettable. "One little nothing moment sticks out in my memory," recalled Liz Moore of Newsday. "I had this sit-down interview with her in Nassau County on her Long Island tour. We were in a side room at one of these catering halls. We finished the interview, I got up to leave, and as I'm walking out of the room, she stretches and yawns. It was a normal human thing to do, but it was so shocking to me to actually see her yawn."

In the book "The Making of the President, 1960," Theodore White pioneered a much-imitated method of observing candidates up close and writing in colorful detail about who they were and how they behaved, not just what they said in their stump speeches. But by 1972, when White was interviewed for "The Boys on the Bus," he mused that the media's intrusion on the candidates' personal moments had gotten out of hand. Recalling the night George McGovern won the Democratic presidential nomination, White said: "There were three different network crews at different times. The still photographers kept coming in, in groups of five. And there were at least six writers sitting in the corner ... We're all sitting there watching him work on his acceptance speech, poor bastard.... All of us are observing him, taking notes like mad, getting all the little details. Which I think I invented as a method of reporting and which I now sincerely regret... Who gives a fuck if the guy had milk and Total (cereal) for breakfast? There's a conflict here: the absolute need of the public to know versus the candidate's need for privacy, which is an equivalent and absolute need. I don't know how you resolve it."

Hillary resolved it for us. We never did get our behind-the-scenes access, and we never found out why. Was it her elaborate first lady security operation? Her own strong personal reserve and high-walled zone of privacy? Her decision? Her advisers' decision? Or just the reality that hers could never be a normal campaign? An AP photographer always rode on the president's plane. I'd ridden on a plane with Al D'Amato and Gov. George Pataki during the '98 Senate campaign, and my colleague Frank Eltman rode on a plane with Lazio and on buses with Pataki and Giuliani during the 2000 Senate race. The candidate doesn't give up all privacy in these situations; there are ground rules involving where the press sits, what's on the record and what's off the record and when it's OK to take pictures. But that, apparently, wasn't good enough for Hillary.

No member of the media ever set foot in Hillary's plane, and we didn't even have pictures of her getting off it. (Not only that, but no member of the press ever set foot in her van, either.) If we landed at the airport with her, we could only assume that the 707 jet, with no mark on it but a code number, was hers. But her staff would time the arrivals so we couldn't see her disembarking, or would spin the plane around upon landing so that the side with the door was facing away from us.

(Keeping us away from the plane also limited discussion of the controversy over who was paying for it. Like presidents and vice presidents who campaign for re-election, Hillary paid only the equivalent of one first-class airfare for each of her trips aboard a plane that cost around $3,000 an hour to operate. She used the government-subsidized jet because of security concerns, but Republicans were always demanding that she reimburse the taxpayers for the entire cost of the flights, and not just what was required under the law.)

All this lack of access was in stark contrast to what the New York media usually got from publicity-hungry politicians. Ed Koch when he was mayor met with the press so many times each day at City Hall that reporters sometimes wondered how he was getting any work done.

Even Giuliani, who had a notoriously antagonistic relationship with the press, gave reporters an opportunity to ask him questions nearly every weekday. That's not to say he made it easy; he didn't. He frequently held the avails in faraway corners of the city while presiding over some other event, instead of at City Hall, where it would be much more convenient for the press to attend. And he often refused to answer the questions he was asked. He also got angry with reporters who asked him about controversial or personal subjects like police brutality or his prostate cancer, for example. But even an angry response or a refusal to respond is something you can report. At least you can let your readers know that, hey, we tried to get the answer to this, and this guy you elected blew up at us or went mum. That observation may in fact give the public as much of a basis for judging their leaders as the actual answer to the question.

Gabe Pressman, a WNBC-TV correspondent who began working in City Hall in 1949 and was still covering politics decades later, once told me Hillary was "the least accessible candidate I had ever covered in New York. I think the Secret Service was not the culprit; I think the campaign itself wanted us to hold back from asking her questions. Is there an avail today? No, maybe tomorrow; we had one yesterday.... The pope has audiences, queens have audiences. Candidates shouldn't have audiences... My experience covering candidates in New York is that they're available. On the other hand, it's White House style.... I think she really believes in her heart that this is the way it's done and that we're an unruly, irreverent bunch."

Pressman blamed the press corps for not making a bigger fuss about the lack of access. "We could have taught her in one day—just say, 'Whaddaya mean, there's no avail?'" he said. But in truth, we did complain, and as time went on, some of us, including me, made it a personal policy to stake her out and shout a question on a day when there was no avail. But only sometimes did she stop to answer.

With Schumer and D'Amato, if we had any complaints about access, it was that there was too much of it. The two of them were a couple of publicity hounds vying to outfox each other. D'Amato, like a lot of politicians, had a system where you could reach him 24 hours a day, seven days a week, by paging a spokesman. He would then personally call back within minutes, even on a Sunday afternoon or late at night, as if he had nothing better to do.

And when I went to write a profile of Schumer, his press secretary, Cathie Levine, who later went to work for Hillary's campaign, not only had him call me at home to chat, but also supplied his mother's phone number so I could interview her. Mama Schumer told me she'd been amazed when her son had gone into politics because, as a little boy, he'd been terribly shy. Somehow I couldn't imagine Howard inviting me to call Hillary's mother to find out what she'd been like as a little girl.

I did get one five-minute phone call from Hillary once during the campaign. It was when I was writing a story about how she was shedding her image as a cold, aloof first lady by sticking around after every event to shake hands, sign autographs, pose for photos and chat. The personal contact really impressed voters, and when I asked Howard for comment, he said he'd have her call me.

"Is that Beth?" came a familiar voice on the other end of the line when it rang at my desk. "This is Hillary Clinton!" I was so shocked that it took me a minute to remember why I'd wanted to speak with her.

A lot of reporters and photographers also complained that they were never sure Hillary knew who they were, or that it took her much longer than the average candidate to get to know them. Part of this was due to our huge numbers, but it was also because she held far fewer avails and often positioned herself physically far away from us, forcing us to shout our questions over the audience. I covered Hillary for months before I was certain that she knew my name. In contrast, just a few weeks after I started covering Schumer, when I started to identify myself before asking a question, he interrupted me to say, "I know exactly who you are."

The Schumer and D'Amato campaigns also always made sure the press corps was fed. If we were on the road, there was a break around lunchtime in a place with restaurants, or sandwiches on the plane. The Lazio campaign was also careful, on most days, to keep the press corps well fed. Only Hillary's campaign would start with an event at 7 or 8 a.m. and keep you going without a break for the next eight hours. "I'm starving!" someone would always be wailing by late afternoon, at which point the driver would feel sorry for us and order pizza by cellphone to be delivered to the van, or we would scrounge around in our bags for snacks and end up passing around a half-eaten bag of cookies or split a bagel four ways as if we were trying to survive the siege of Leningrad. I took to packing sandwiches wrapped in tin foil, like a kid on a school trip; AP photographer Suzanne Plunkett and I lived for an entire week at one point on my egg salad sandwiches as we catapulted from one Hillary event to another.

Once Lazio started making Hillary look bad in this department, not only by providing food but also by renting a big press bus equipped with electrical outlets for laptops, cable TV and a bathroom, Hillary said something to us about how much more money his campaign had than hers, and that's why he had superior accommodations. "I'd buy you an ocean liner if I could!" she said grandly. But in truth every news organization was billed for the transportation and other amenities, except for the occasional box of doughnuts thrown to us by a sympathetic staff member.

Occasionally, though, the first lady herself took pity on us. Once when we arrived at a synagogue on Long Island where she was making a speech to a women's group, we could see into the temple kitchen from the parking lot and began salivating over the nice sit-down lunch being prepared for the ladies. Hillary's van pulled up a minute later, and as she got out, she looked over and saw us leering at the food.

"What's the matter, aren't they going to feed you?" she called out with a laugh. It was sometime in April of 2000, and a new poll that day had shown her surging ahead of Giuliani, who was then still in the race, and we had all noticed that she was in an incredibly sunny mood.

A few minutes after we got inside, one of the hosts of the event brought over two huge baskets overflowing with bagels and rolls, compliments of Hillary.

When the event was over and we piled back into our van, the driver turned around and handed us another basket chock-full of candy and cookies.

"Where did this come from?" someone asked. The driver said it had been given to Hillary as a gift by the synagogue, and she had had one of her aides turn it over to us.

"You're kidding," I said. The driver insisted it was true, and I dug in. As each reporter climbed into the van and was offered a chocolate, the story was repeated and was met with the same incredulous reaction: "No way." "Tell me the truth." "Are you sure?" "Who told you that?" It was like Halloween on the press van, and none of us could believe that Hillary was being so nice to us. Who knew what might be next? More press conferences? Personal interviews? Phone calls returned promptly by her staff? We could only dream. In fact, just a few months later she actually ventured onto a bus carrying the press on one of her upstate tours, chatted for 20 minutes, and personally handed out cookies from a local bakery with her image on them in colorful icing. I wasn't in attendance that day, but it was the talk of the press corps for a long time.

In "The Boys on the Bus," Crouse complained about how Nixon's press secretary, Ron Ziegler, drove reporters nuts with his refusals to give out the most basic information, and his red herrings—announcements about obscure developments that were specifically designed to divert attention from what he knew was the news of the day. At one point, Ziegler told the reporters to form a committee to come up with a rule for how the press conferences should end. Ziegler felt that the system in place, in which a wire-service reporter ended the news conferences with a singsong "Thank you," had become too chaotic with some reporters continuing to ask questions after the "Thank you" was uttered.

I couldn't help but think that those guys didn't know how good they had it. Hillary's press conferences also always ended with a "Thank you, Mrs. Clinton." But it wasn't a reporter who got to say it. It was Howard.

rrounded by family and fellow Democrats, Hillary Rodham Clinton announces her candidacy r the U.S. Senate in Purchase, N.Y. Supporting the first lady, from left, are Rep. Charles angel, D-N.Y., Rep. Nita Lowey, D-N.Y., Sen. Charles Schumer, D-N.Y., Sen. Daniel Patrick oynihan, D-N.Y., President Clinton, Chelsea Clinton and Mrs. Clinton's mother, Dorothy odham, Feb. 6, 2000. (AP Photo/Kathy Willens)

Dressed as first lady Hillary Rodham Clinton and Yasser Arafat, protestors outside the Clintons' home in Chappaqua, N.Y., to challenge the first lady's position on Israeli-Palestinian relations, March 12, 2000. (AP Photo/Stephen Chernin)

The controversial moment when first lady Hillary Rodham Clinton, left, kissed Sol Arafat, wife of Palestinian leader Yasser Arafat, during a visit to the West Bank town of Ramallah at a ceremony to commemorate a $3.8 million U.S. grant for health care in the West Bank and Gaza Strip, Nov. 11, 1999. (AP Photo/Ruth Fremson)

ABOVE: Clinton's Senate campaign spokesman Howard Wolfson watches a studio monitor as Clinton, in background, appears during the "Today" show's town hall meeting in New York, May 11, 2000. (AP Photo/Bebeto Matthews)

RIGHT: Clinton dances with New York's Bronx Borough President Fernando Ferrer during the Puerto Rican Day parade in New York. Clinton was cheered as she danced to the song "Soy Puro Borincano," which translates "Pure Puerto Rican," June 11, 2000. (AP Photos/Bebeto Matthews)

U.S. Senate candidate Hillary Rodham Clinton sings during the Mass of Installation for Archbishop Edward Egan at St. Patrick's Cathedral in New York while her opposition, Rep. Rick Lazio, R-N.Y., stands behind, June 19, 2000. (AP Photo/Peter Morgan)

Senate candidate Clinton bowls during a fund-raiser for St. Pius V School, at the Leisure Time bowling alley in New York's Port Authority bus terminal, July 17, 2000. (AP Photo/Beth A. Keiser)

President Bill Clinton and Hillary embrace during the New York State Senate 2000 luncheon, New York City, July 2, 2000. (AP Photo/Pablo Martinez Monsivais)

Senate candidate Hillary Rodham Clinton is greeted by fans at Cornell University in Ithaca, N.Y., Oct. 28, 2000. (AP Photo/ Jim McKnight)

New York U.S. Senate-elect Hillary Rodham Clinton celebrates with President Clinton and daughter Chelsea during her victory rally in New York, Nov. 7, 2000. (AP Photo/Ron Edmonds)

CHAPTER 6

What's the Lead?

The Colorado school shooting at Columbine took place in April 1999, as Hillary's Senate campaign began to unfold. Then as now, gun violence in general was making headlines, but back then, the gun control movement was growing and there was far less pushback from gun owners. Like many other liberals at the time, Hillary Clinton wasn't shy about supporting gun control, and she has remained a strong proponent. In contrast, many other politicians have moderated their stances as gun rights supporters and the National Rifle Association have become more powerful politically in the 21st century.

Hillary even scored a point over Vermont Sen. Bernie Sanders during a debate in the 2016 race when she questioned his support for gun control, one of the few issues where Hillary is to the left of Sanders. He's a socialist, but he's from a rural state where hunting culture is big.

I wonder if any politician in the U.S. today—Hillary or anybody else—would dare visit a school and lead the kids in a pledge against guns, the way Hillary did in the account that follows from the year 2000.

• • •

We were riding around suburban Rockland County in March 2000 in a van with four rows of seats packed so tight with reporters that it felt like a city bus at rush hour. Everyone was busy mumbling into cellphones, shuffling paper in skinny, spiral-bound reporter's notebooks and fast-forwarding cassette recorders with a high-pitched squeak. We used the tapes to double-check the quotes we scribbled down illegibly as Hillary talked to the kids inside the Valley

Cottage School. And we glumly called our offices with the usual disappointing news: There was no news.

No, we told our editors, Hillary's not doing an avail.

No, she didn't attack Giuliani.

No, she still hadn't made any comment, four days after a verdict came down acquitting four white police officers in the death of an African immigrant, Amadou Diallo, whom they'd shot as he stood in the doorway of his home. The officers mistakenly believed the wallet Diallo was holding was a gun.

And, no, she hadn't uttered a word about the story that was on every front page in America that day: the fatal shooting of one 6-year-old by another in a Michigan school.

"So what's the lead?" a voice called out from somewhere in the van.

In the van was the usual group of print reporters for the New York Post, Daily News, New York Times, and me, for AP, plus producers for NBC and ABC; a couple of still photographers; and one of Hillary's press aides, Karen Dunn. Behind us were a couple more vans carrying TV crews, and ahead of us were Hillary and her aides in her van, a shiny black-and-gray custom Ford with tinted windows and white Washington, D.C., plates that begin with the letters AR, as in "Arkansas." (It would be months before she'd switch to New York plates.) Her van had a raised roof a foot high, and I always wondered what was stored inside. Her aides insisted it just provided extra headroom, but I couldn't help thinking that maybe there was a nuclear hot line up there, just in case the president caught a ride with her. AP photographer Suzanne Plunkett called it the Hillary Mystery Van. Bob Hardt from the Post and Joel Siegel from the Daily News called it HRC Speedwagon, a reference to an old rock band, REO Speedwagon.

I became obsessed with peeking into the van, just because it was so completely off-limits to us. One day, looking through the window on the driver's side at the backseat where Hillary sat, I noticed a huge, ugly plastic shopping bag from the Duane Reade drugstore. It appeared to be overflowing with items that I could not make out through the tinted glass, but I found it amusing to imagine one of Hillary's aides running into Duane Reade like everybody else in New York, filling a shopping basket with lipstick and Tylenol and little packs of tissues and nail files and panty hose and breath mints and Band-Aids and God knows what else. Even a first lady has to wipe her nose sometimes.

Then, of course, I felt like a media vulture. Jeez, couldn't the woman make a trip to the drugstore without me trying to snoop around on her?

Back in the van in Rockland County, a voice was insistently repeating "What's the lead?" Suddenly the low volume changed to a commanding tone from the speaker, who'd never ridden with us before. She didn't know any of us, but we all knew her: Mary McGrory, the legendary political columnist for the Washington Post. She was old enough to be my grandmother, and although her writing and reporting were as sharp as ever, and I would be the first to admit, better than mine, age had taken its toll on her mobility. It was so hard for her to get in and out of the van that other reporters had to bodily boost her up from the ground. This would be utterly humiliating for anyone else, but for McGrory, it was just another reason to respect her. She was already 55 when Crouse included her as one of the only women in "The Boys on the Bus," and she was still slogging along the campaign trail 28 years later, when most of her peers long ago took desk jobs, retired, went into public relations or became journalism professors.

Still, her question, "What's the lead?" went unanswered. There was an embarrassed silence for a minute or two. The daily newspaper reporters never shared their leads. It just wasn't done. Why was she asking? Surely Mary McGrory didn't need any help in figuring out the lead.

But I didn't care. Half my colleagues already heard my lead as I dumped my notes by cellphone to another reporter back at AP's Rockefeller Center headquarters. Everybody on the van would see my story on the wire before their own stories were filed, so secrets were pointless.

I didn't even need to check my notes to answer McGrory's question.

"Hillary Rodham Clinton led several hundred children at a Rockland County elementary school in a pledge against gun violence," I recited from memory in a monotone. A couple of giggles, a wave of relief; now nobody else had to divulge his or her approach to today's story.

"Thank you," McGrory said grandly.

"Hey, I'm AP. I've got no secrets," I said, shrugging. Even so, I felt just slightly ashamed that there was no more news than that. We wanted the lead to be Hillary's comment on one of the top two news stories—the Diallo acquittals or the Michigan classroom shooting. But we couldn't write about her comments on these stories because we didn't have her comments on these stories. We'd been 3 feet away from her as she chatted with kids inside the Valley Cottage school, but somehow none of us had managed to ask her a question.

So instead, the story had to be about this anti-gun pledge. It wasn't a bad lead; Hillary had asked a group of fifth-graders in the auditorium to promise that they'd never touch weapons or use them in anger, saying, "Would you do that as good citizens for us?" The children shouted "Yes" and "I promise" in response. It made a nice little sound bite for TV and radio, and at least it was about gun violence on a day when gun violence was in the news. But it just wasn't explicitly enough about 6-year-olds killing each other to be widely used.

"What's wrong with us?" Eileen Murphy, a producer for ABC, had lamented as we'd stood in the school, close enough to touch Hillary, stupidly waiting for her to do what we knew she never would: Just turn to us and make this story, this trip, this boring day, worthwhile with a sentence or two about the real news on everyone's mind. "We're still treating her like a first lady!"

She was right. If Hillary had been any other candidate, we would have walked right up to her and asked her what needed to be asked. But we'd been told there'd be no avail today, and we'd accepted it. That didn't prevent me from feeling slightly humiliated.

I was so worn down and so exasperated by the lack of access and the lack of news in this campaign that I'd given up fighting, and no reporter wants to admit that. I kept trying to rationalize what was happening, telling myself, "It's not me. It's her." Any other candidate would recognize the news of the day and capitalize on it. Any other candidate would realize that the press and the voters expect you to weigh in on whatever's making headlines, whether it has to do with the office you're seeking or not. It's how people figure out who you are and what your values are.

But other candidates weren't surrounded by Secret Service agents.

Other candidates wouldn't stand a chance of attracting an entourage of reporters if all they were doing was shlepping to a suburban elementary school. Other candidates weren't the only first lady in history to ever run for office.

Some of the reporters covering Hillary had also spent time covering Sen. John McCain's presidential campaign, and as we rode away from the Rockland County school where we'd had no access to the first lady, we couldn't help but compare her to McCain, whose access never ended. McCain talked all day long with reporters on his Straight Talk Express bus; he talked so much that he sometimes said things he shouldn't have, and that's why the media loved him. Just a month after Hillary visited the Valley Cottage School, McCain, a Republican supporting Giuliani's bid against Hillary, told students at a forum at Columbia University that if Hillary made it to the Senate, "She would be a star of the quality that has not been seen in the Senate since Bobby Kennedy was elected senator from the state of New York." It was hard to imagine any other Republican saying anything like that about Hillary, even though in private they probably all agreed.

Next stop was a hotel luncheon with a Rockland County business group.

As she blathered on about issuing technology bonds to help communities finance high-speed Internet connections, I noticed that most of my colleagues had stopped taking notes. This lady was all substance and no sound bites.

Then we piled back into the van for a return trip to Manhattan, only to have her aide suddenly announce a surprise stop: a striking nurses' picket line at Nyack Hospital.

This seemingly innocuous news was met with groans, whines and muttering. Another hour before we could get back to our offices.

Another event with no news. Another example of how disorganized her press office was.

But soon it became clear that while the visit to the picket line was a surprise to us, the striking nurses had been told beforehand. As the vans pulled up where the nurses were rallying, I could see that some of them were wearing "Hillary" buttons and carrying "Hillary" signs. Her press office had known they were taking us here, but they hadn't told us in advance.

I was angry that we hadn't gotten an opportunity to ask her for a comment earlier and angry that the schedule was being screwed around with. I was determined to get close enough to her to ask something. I moved through the crowd of nurses as she did, keeping her directly in my line of sight. At one point, I stopped to get the name of a nurse who'd asked her a question, and when I tried to reposition myself near Hillary, a Secret Service agent who'd seen me dozens of times in the past put his hand out and ordered me to move away. If it hadn't happened to me 50 times before, I would have been outraged. After all, I had a credential issued by the NYPD; they had my photo and Social Security number on file. Any nutcase could walk right up to her, and they're acting like I'm the threat. But arguing with him would have been a waste of time, so I simply crossed the street, ran ahead a quarter of a block, stood where I knew she was headed, then rejoined the pack when she reached me.

Her van was moving up the street along with her entourage. Obviously she was preparing to leave. I was a foot away from her, so I caught her eye and seized my chance. "Gun violence, Mrs. Clinton?" I shouted. "Can you give us your thoughts on gun violence?" It was too noisy and chaotic to ask a complicated question specifically about the Michigan shooting; the idea here was to throw out a phrase, as simple and loud as possible, to grab her attention. If she had anything at all to say on the Michigan shooting, this was her opportunity.

She looked right at me for a second and hesitated. I could see that she'd heard me. Then she lowered her eyes from mine, made a slight gesture with her hand as if to say, "I'm done here," and got in her van without a word.

I was disappointed and even felt a little stupid. But at least I couldn't kick myself any longer for not having attempted to get her. Eileen was right; we shouldn't be treating her like a first lady. Even if she wasn't going to answer me, from now on I was going to ask.

The next day, Mary McGrory's column about the trip contained two unforgettable lines: "A splendid elementary teacher was plainly lost when Hillary married Bill and politics" and "The ladies on the Hillary press van ... call her 'the un-McCain.'" I wasn't sure whether any of us had actually uttered that phrase, or whether she had simply captured what we were feeling more articulately than we could say it ourselves.

That afternoon Hillary was scheduled to be interviewed on WCBS-TV by Marcia Kramer. Marcia could be a bulldog in a one-on-one interview. Her claim to fame, in fact, was with Hillary's husband in 1992, when she'd pinned him down on his previously elusive responses to questions about his marijuana usage. "I never broke the laws of my country" gave way, in Marcia's deft handling, to his admission that while he'd once put a joint to his mouth, he'd never actually inhaled.

So I was hoping for a similar bombshell as I arrived at the WCBS studio to watch the taping. Gregg Birnbaum from the Post was there, too, but none of the other regulars had bothered to show up. They could just as easily watch it from their offices, but Gregg and I figured it was worth going to the station on the off chance that we'd catch Hillary outside. As the interview wore on, it was clear no news would be committed. Outside, afterward, we looked for the Speedwagon, but she'd already taken off. Then we spotted Howard and another press aide, Karen Finney.

Gregg started to give Howard a hard time about the fact that it had been five days since the Diallo verdict and we still hadn't had a chance to ask her for a comment, not to mention the fact that there hadn't been any other news coming out of the Hillary campaign in a while.

"What about yesterday?" Howard said, referring to the Valley Cottage School event.

"There was no news in that!" Gregg said.

"Hey, I read a nice little story on the AP wire about it," Howard said with a smile.

Of course, Howard knew that a nice little story about Hillary leading children in pledges against gun violence just wasn't news in the New York Post, the city's most conservative paper. The paper's editorial cartoons typically portrayed Hillary on a broomstick; and while the Post ran the photo of her kissing Suha Arafat as the "wood," newspaper jargon for the front page, the paper's exclusive photo of Lazio grinning ear to ear as he shook Yasser Arafat's hand was deemed unworthy of page 1 and appeared inside instead.

I decided to ask Howard about the Million Mom March, an anti-gun protest planned for Mother's Day in Washington, D.C. I'd been seeing Million Mom March sign-up sheets at my older son's school and at our local synagogue, and it seemed like the type of event that would be a natural for Hillary.

"Million Mom March?" Howard asked. "What's that?"

I explained and added that I'd called the organizers in Washington, and they'd told me that in an effort to keep it nonpartisan, they didn't want politicians to speak at the rally, but they had invited Hillary to take part in the march and hadn't heard back from her office.

"Hillary's a mom," Howard mused. "She could march. I'll find out and get back to you."

Howard frequently offered to find things out and get back to people, but he often did not follow through. It wasn't that he was lazy or inefficient, it was just that he didn't have time to respond to everyone. His pager and cellphone were constantly going off; he often started his day at dawn by buying the papers and ended it after the 11 p.m. news. When he was in the office, he was continuously both on the phone and the computer, simultaneously answering calls and emails from the dozens of media outlets clamoring for a little piece of Hillary.

Of course, when he didn't like something someone had written, he'd find them in an instant and complain vigorously by phone or email. Other times he'd actually call to say he liked a story. He once called me up to compliment a lead I'd written for a Hillary story, then added, "You know, it would be even better if..." Needless to say, I had no intention of rewriting my lead based on his suggestions.

He also had a dry sense of humor and was generally calm in the face of small crises. Once when he was holding a news conference in City Hall Park, a bedraggled, disturbed homeless man walked over, stood next to him, and started to babble. Howard didn't miss a beat. He looked the man in the eye, smiled, and said, "Would you mind just waiting a minute till I finish?" The man took a step back and did just that. AP photographer Bebeto Matthews took a picture of Howard holding court with the homeless man, and another photographer later presented a copy of it to Hillary.

In other ways, however, Howard seemed a bit eccentric. He was allergic to chocolate, nuts and 100 other things and was often sick or inexplicably injured, such as the time he hurt his foot stumbling in a bookstore or the time he showed up at a press conference, his face red and swollen from an allergic reaction. He was terrified of flying and would take the train or drive to upstate cities hours from Manhattan to avoid taking a plane to Hillary's events. He was notorious for paying little attention to his appearance and walked around for the longest time with a huge hole in his shoe. Probably if I had known him personally, in the fuller context of his life, some of these quirks might have faded into the background. But knowing him only as Hillary's protector and defender meant that on any given day my interaction with Howard was limited to his answering a question about Hillary while I noticed that he had a cold or a limp. If nothing else, those small quirks humanized Howard and somehow made it just a little bit easier to have a mostly cordial working relationship with him. He was regarded far less fondly by reporters who dealt with him when Hillary ran for president in 2008, when the door on communication with the press was shut even tighter than it was in the Senate race. Still, it was always a bit of a revelation for me to see him on TV during the 2008 campaign or in subsequent years when he worked for Mayor Michael Bloomberg (a Republican to boot). Howard seemed so smooth and confident in those later roles. The guy with hives and a hole in his shoe, who was as in the dark about what Hillary was doing in 2000 as we were, he was gone.

In contrast to Howard, there was a group of women on Hillary's staff that I often thought of in my head as "the lovelies" because all of them had beautiful smiles and charming personalities. In fact, when Howard recruited Karen Finney to work with him as a press aide, he told her simply, "You're charming. I'm not."

At the time, Finney was working as chief of staff to the CEO of Scholastic. She'd previously worked for five years in the Clinton White House, ending up as the first lady's deputy press secretary, before escaping to a semi-normal life in the private sector, a life where, as she put it, she actually had time to buy groceries and go out with her friends. She went to Scholastic never intending to return to politics, but Howard and Hillary talked her into it.

Karen Dunn, whom Howard had brought in from U.S. Rep. Nita Lowey's staff, was already working on Hillary's campaign when Finney was hired. Dunn, who is white and 5 feet tall, was momentarily concerned that having two Karens on staff would be confusing. "I don't think that will be a problem," Howard said. "Karen Finney is a 6-foot-tall black woman." I sometimes felt like the first lady had purposely surrounded herself with all these warm, sweet, pretty young women: the Karens; her two blond personal assistants, Kelly Craighead and Allison Stein; and later another press aide, Cathie Levine, almost as a foil for the largely humorless Secret Service agents who were always telling us where we couldn't stand.

While my relationship with the Karens was generally one of light, friendly banter, probably from all those hours we spent riding around in the vans together, I sometimes felt paranoid about my dealings with Howard, and I was not the only member of the press corps to experience this insecurity. When he didn't get back to you about something, did that mean he was ignoring you, or had he just forgotten? Ellen Wulfhorst of Reuters summed it up this way: "I started to think Howard wasn't talking to me. But then I thought, 'How would I know the difference?'"

In other words, most of us had become accustomed to being blown off by him, and you couldn't take it personally. For example, standing outside the WCBS studios that day and asking him about the Million Mom March, I could tell immediately that my query had landed in the dead-mail slot in his mind. No one was on deadline about it. No one was accusing Hillary of doing anything evil. If he heard anything about it on his end, he would get back to me, but I knew he wasn't going to go out of his way to pin it down.

So I was peeved to hear that two days later, when Hillary finally got around to holding a press conference, her first in a week, she announced that she was going to take part in the Million Mom March! Now it was out there for everyone to write about. (In the media business, nothing is newsworthy when everyone knows it.) Since I asked about it first, he should have told me ahead of the pack.

I was angry and confused. Had Howard been lying to me? Had he really not known? And why, since this had turned out to be important enough for Hillary to make an announcement about, hadn't he followed up on it? But I decided not to confront him about it. Instead, I figured I'd just wait until the next time he called to complain about something I'd written and bring it up then.

I didn't have to wait long. That Sunday, Hillary was making what her campaign had billed as a "major" speech at Riverside Church, a liberal and politically active church near Columbia University. Riverside was one of the obligatory stops for politicians on the campaign trail, along with ringing the opening bell on Wall Street, eating at a Jewish deli and appearing at the 92nd Street Y.

Hillary had traded in her black pantsuit for her going-to-church skirt. Her speech turned out to be a lawyerly appeal for better relations between police and the citizens they protect. She referred repeatedly to a "false choice" city officials had made between bringing crime down and treating New Yorkers with respect. She had made a similar speech the weekend before at a conference for Dominican New Yorkers, so I wasn't sure why this speech was billed as a big deal. From Riverside we headed in a press van to Queens, where Hillary was marching in a small St. Patrick's Day parade five days before the big parade March 17 on Fifth Avenue. Unlike the big event, this smaller march in Queens had decided to allow an Irish gay group to take part.

Hillary's new line was that she would march in the big parade to show support for the Irish peace process, and she'd take part in the small parade to show support for the Irish gay group. "It's a case of competing values," she'd repeatedly said.

A lot of reporters hate covering parades because they're chaotic and exhausting. You have to fight with the cops to stand where you want; you have to walk a couple of miles, regardless of the weather; and you have to pay attention every second on the off chance that something dreadful happens. I once covered a St. Patrick's Day parade with Mayor David Dinkins in which beer bottles went whizzing by his head, and mine, and that taught me that parades can create a lot of news.

But as I tried to get near Hillary, I realized the police were insisting that the media not walk in the middle of the street with the marchers, but instead stay behind the blue NYPD barricades that had been set up all along the parade route to keep spectators on the sidewalk. Our press credentials specifically state that the bearer "is entitled to pass police and fire lines wherever formed," so at first I ignored the officers who kept telling me to get out of the line of march. Finally a sergeant came over and ordered me in no uncertain terms out of the parade route. The AP, the Times, the Daily News, and the New York Press Club had just negotiated an agreement with the city over the police department's failure to honor our press passes. The pact stipulated that the NYPD would, in the future, allow us to cross police lines unless there was an imminent danger, like a fire or a hostage situation. But now I had this sergeant in my face. I asked him whether he was familiar with the agreement, but he simply repeated his order that I get on the sidewalk.

The AP later protested the incident at a meeting with police brass, but for me to argue it out on the street would have meant having my press pass confiscated. That was a hassle I didn't have time for, so I did as he asked. One by one every reporter and camera crew was relegated to the same area as the spectators.

But the sidewalk turned out to be a decent vantage point for the story that presented itself. A band of hecklers was walking along the sidewalk, following Hillary and booing her. "Go home!" they were shouting. "Carpetbagger! Go back to Arkansas!" I began interviewing them and discovered that a lot of them were not from the neighborhood, but had made a special trip from Brooklyn or Manhattan for the sole purpose of heckling Hillary. One woman who told me she hated Hillary because she'd been a doormat for Bill's sexual escapades went running down the street, screaming at the first lady at the top of her lungs, "You're an enabler!"

But as I walked along, I realized that while the traveling band of hecklers was loud, an awful lot of less audible boos and nasty remarks were coming from spectators who did live in the neighborhood and had simply turned out to watch the parade. This was a story. Hillary's first foray on the streets of New York City had turned into something of a fiasco. In fairness, she was receiving just as many cheers and applause as boos, and she appeared unfazed by the negative reception. But no one had expected this level of hostility. This was Hillary's first full-blown, unprotected exposure to the masses, and it wasn't pretty. I called my office to dump my notes.

Shortly after the story moved on the wire, Howard called. I could hear that he was using his deadpan, formal tone of voice as The Man Who Protects Hillary from Bad Publicity. "I am shocked that on a day when the first lady makes a major policy announcement regarding the police and race relations, The Associated Press would choose to lead with a parade," he said.

I had no intention of changing the lead, but as long as I had him on the phone, I figured it was time to talk about the little grievance I'd been nursing.

"Imagine how shocked I was to find out, with the rest of the world, that Hillary was marching in the Million Mom March, after I specifically asked you about it and you promised to get back to me," I said, trying to strike the same tone of voice.

"Oh. So this is payback?"

"No, it's not payback. I've just been wondering why you didn't get back to me about it, and this seems like a good time to bring it up."

"I honestly didn't know. When she started talking about the Million Mom March at the press conference, it was a total surprise to me."

In other words, he wasn't keeping information away from us. Hillary was keeping information away from him.

We had a few more polite go-rounds about the day's story and said goodbye. I knew he'd be as friendly to me the next time I saw him as he always was, and even though I hadn't changed my story in response to his complaint, I wanted him to feel that he could always make a case for his point of view. Every now and then he'd point out an error or ask to have the campaign's point of view portrayed in a different way, and after all, I wanted to be fair, I wanted to be accurate and I was willing to listen to feedback. On the other hand, I was not a mouthpiece for the campaign. Just because Hillary's people think she's made news doesn't mean I have to agree.

When I went into work the next day, I was surprised to see that the Post, the Times and the Daily News had agreed with Howard and led with the Riverside speech. I agonized about it for a little while, but in the end I decided I'd made the right choice for the AP. I was writing for an audience of upstaters and out-of-staters, and a statement made 10 days after the Diallo verdict just wasn't that important to my readers, especially when it sounded like a retread of what I'd led with the previous weekend when she'd spoken at a Dominican conference. On the other hand, for the first lady to walk down a street and get booed seemed like news to me.

A few days later, Hillary had a 5 p.m. event at a gay community center in Greenwich Village, but when I got there, it was running very late. It was the day after Super Tuesday, I was tired from having worked late the night before, and I wanted to see my boys, so I decided to skip it.

I collected a few phone numbers from people in the audience so I could make some calls later and find out what had happened, and I headed home.

When I walked in the door, I saw my answering machine blinking. Bebeto Matthews, the AP photographer, had called to let me know Hillary had been heckled. A couple of people at the gay meeting had started screaming at her because she had agreed to march in the main St. Patrick's Day parade, which excluded the gay contingent. Damn it! I was angry with myself and slightly panicked that I had missed this. I was responsible for making sure that Hillary was always covered; then finally news happens and I'm not there. But Bebeto had taken some notes, gotten a quote and a name, and I was able to reach some of the people whose numbers I'd taken. I managed to piece together a little story even though I hadn't been there.

She had apparently handled the situation well, asking the hecklers to allow her to deliver her prepared remarks, and then discussing their concerns afterward. She explained that while she was disappointed that the parade does not include a gay contingent, she wanted to support the Irish peace process. She repeated her "competing values" line.

Before I called the story in to my office, I beeped Howard.

"Did you guys run a tape?" I asked when he called back, knowing that the press staff often carried a microcassette recorder to take down her statements.

"Yeah," he replied.

"Can you get me a quote off of it?"

" No."

"Why not?"

"She took it with her."

"Well, can't you get it?"

"Not until tomorrow."

Gee, thanks. It was my own fault for not sticking around. On the other hand, I was home with my kids. It was a case of MY competing values: Hillary versus Danny and Nathaniel. I called my office, dictated a short story, and made dinner.

The day after I missed the hecklers at the gay meeting, Peggy Noonan's new book came out: "The Case Against Hillary Clinton." Yet another Hillary hate book; there were so many, it was hard to keep track. Noonan spends part of the book talking about Clinton victims, and after the last few weeks, I was starting to feel like a Clinton victim myself. When I followed Hillary around all day, there was no news. The one time I skipped an event, news happened. If I reported something unflattering, Howard complained. If I wanted to report something that made her look good, the Million Mom March or the way she handled the gay meeting, he couldn't help. Noonan's book contended that the Clintons simply hate the media, don't trust them and stonewall on giving out even the most benign and basic information. That would certainly explain what I was experiencing.

It might also explain why it sometimes seemed that Howard was being kept in the dark. Why tell your press staff what's going on and take the chance that they might actually tell the press?

Finally the main St. Patrick's Day parade was at hand. Hillary held a brief news conference before joining the march to restate her "competing values" line, explaining why she was marching in the parade even though she sympathized with the gay marchers who were being excluded. She was wearing a green scarf, and all along the parade route, volunteer supporters wearing "Hillary" pins with little shamrocks were in place to cheer.

But it became obvious almost immediately that this was going to be an even bigger fiasco than the Queens St. Pat's parade. The booing was loud, strong and persistent. It was so bad that at no point did she veer over to the sidelines to shake hands with spectators. There were a lot of people from the suburbs, a lot of Catholics, a lot of Giuliani supporters, and a lot of people related to cops; this was not a Hillary crowd. The cries of "Go back to Arkansas!" and "Carpetbagger!" were so pervasive that the radio reporters didn't need to seek anybody out for a sound bite—they just walked along the parade route holding out their microphones to catch the ambient sound. As for the problem we'd had with the cops at the previous parade in Queens, it had disappeared. We were allowed to march in the street with Hillary without being hassled.

Hillary, meanwhile, kept a smile frozen on her face and left her arm up in a friendly wave for the entire 2 miles of the parade route. She had to hear the boos and see the angry looks she was getting, but she never let her reaction show.

I went back to the office and spoke with the reporter who'd covered Giuliani. The mayor had been cheered the whole way and spent so much time shaking hands with supporters that he'd had to take little sprints every block or so to catch back up with the line of march.

I knew what the lead was. And this time I knew Howard wouldn't be calling to complain.

CHAPTER 7

Goodbye Rudy, Hello Rick

I'm often asked whether Hillary would have won if Rudy Giuliani had stayed in the race. I honestly think so, and believe the mayor dropped out because he knew his chances were fading.

It's easy to think of Giuliani as a one-dimensional hero for New York: He is credited with cleaning up the city in the 1990s and making it safer, and even his enemies would admit that he provided calm and inspiring leadership in the city's darkest hours after the 9/11 attacks.

But it's important to remember how ambivalent many voters felt about him when Hillary launched her Senate campaign. His brusque personality played better at City Hall than upstate or in Washington. He was a "my way or the highway" kind of mayor, and that's not necessarily the right personality for the U.S. Senate. He was also blamed for worsening racial tensions around the city, and he'd made it abundantly clear that he had zero interest in campaigning upstate. Finally, the public disintegration of his marriage, as his wife accused him of not one but two affairs, managed to make Hillary and Bill's relationship look pretty good by comparison.

• • •

A story in the New York Post on April 27, 2000, reported that Mayor Rudolph Giuliani was undergoing tests for prostate cancer. It wasn't a front-page story; he wasn't fatally ill, he was just having a test. But shortly after I arrived at work that morning, the mayor's press office announced a news conference. Our City Hall reporter, Timothy Williams, would cover it in person, and I would watch it on

TV and put a few paragraphs on the wire ahead of Timothy's more comprehensive story. In the meantime, I called Bruce Teitelbaum, spokesman for Giuliani's Senate campaign and a tense man under the best of circumstances.

He answered his cellphone immediately but sounded miserable.

"Hullo," he muttered. I identified myself and asked if he could give us any information about whether the mayor's health was going to affect his Senate campaign. Slowly, deliberately and glumly, he replied, "I ... have ... nothing ... to ... say."

The press conference took place in the Blue Room at City Hall. In his usual businesslike mode, the mayor stood at the podium and said he had prostate cancer but that it was in an early stage and was treatable.

The very first question was how this would affect his Senate campaign. I and many others assumed he'd say it wouldn't affect it all. After all, Yankees manager Joe Torre had an equally demanding and stressful job, and he'd led the Yankees to a World Series victory while undergoing prostate cancer treatment. Bob Dole had prostate cancer, and five years later he ran for president.

But Giuliani said he wasn't sure. "I don't think it's fair to answer questions about the Senate race right now," he said. "Should I do it? Would I be able to do it the right way? I hope that's the case, but I don't know."

That "I don't know" was bigger news than anyone expected. Why would any politician in a cutthroat race like this one where he and Hillary had been neck and neck in the polls for months admit that a treatable illness might force him to drop out?

He talked about his father, who had died of prostate cancer, saying, "I think about my father every day of my life." And he claimed that the illness had given him a new perspective on life. Was the cold, brusque, take-no-prisoners Rudy morphing into someone kinder and gentler?

A lot of reporters who covered the mayor believed that he was an extremely careful and calculating politician, that his temper tantrums at the press and sometimes callous remarks about people and institutions he despised (like when he suggested blowing up the Board of Education) were not impulsive, uncontrollable outbursts but deliberate maneuvers. So there were two ways to look at his admission that he was uncertain about remaining in the Senate race: Either he screwed up by answering honestly when he should have denied that it would affect his aspirations, or he was making a play for voters' sympathy because Hillary had effectively made his belligerent personality an issue in the race. She'd contended over and over that his inability to compromise and get along with people who disagree with him made him unfit for the Senate, a place where you can't get anything accomplished if you don't make deals with your enemies. We had a lot of fun in the van quoting Hillary's favorite declarations on the subject. "I reject the politics of division and destruction!" we'd say as dramatically as we could. "I want to lift people up, not pull them down!"

But it was a smart tack for her to take on his personality, because she couldn't attack his competency. Too many voters gave him credit for bringing down crime, cleaning up Times Square and making New York a more livable place. Those of us who lived here couldn't deny that squeegee men no longer stalked cars at stoplights, subway riders no longer sneaked cigarettes in the stations and 42nd Street theaters no longer advertised peep shows.

In a city where Democrats outnumber Republican voters 5 to 1, Giuliani had swamped his Democratic opponent, Ruth Messinger, in his 1997 re-election campaign. Yet he wasn't completely acceptable as a hero in his own party, largely because of his liberal views on abortion, gun control and gay rights. He'd also crossed party lines at times to endorse Democrats who he thought offered more for city residents than Republicans; his endorsement of Democrat Mario Cuomo against Republican George Pataki in 1994 for New York governor caused a rift between him and Pataki that had never healed.

But the same personality that allowed Giuliani to do whatever he thought was right, regardless of public opinion or political alliances, also provided fodder for Hillary's contention that he'd have trouble forming alliances in the Senate and that he was not sensitive enough to the concerns of minorities and the poor.

Some pundits suggested that Giuliani was trying to counteract that impression by using the cancer announcement to portray himself as vulnerable. But others said he had made a fatal campaign error—his fundraising operation (which had brought in $20 million already, with $9 million still unspent when his cancer was made public) would be crippled by the uncertainty and voters would view him as damaged goods.

There was a third school of thought. What if Giuliani really didn't want to continue the Senate race? What if he'd gotten into it thinking it would be an amusing cakewalk over Hillary, only to find that it was more like a wrestling match that required a lot more of his time than he wanted to devote to it? What if he had no interest in spending the rest of the year hobnobbing in upstate diners and county fairs and factories?

What if he was tired of the fundraising and the polls and having the national media bugging him just as much as the local press did? Hillary had set a goal of visiting every one of New York's 62 counties and had been swooping in with her entourage to obscure little places like Penn Yan, a tiny Finger Lakes town whose previous claim to fame was being home to the world's largest buckwheat pancake. Giuliani, in contrast, couldn't even be bothered to show up for a "Women for Rudy" fundraiser that had been scheduled in Rochester a few weeks before his cancer announcement. When the Yankees' opening game got rescheduled for the same day as the Rochester event, he bagged the ladies' lunch for the stadium. Republicans and upstaters had been grumbling ever since that the mayor wasn't showing a lot of enthusiasm for campaigning north of the Bronx. Maybe the prostate cancer was the excuse he'd been looking for to bow out.

When the mayor's press conference was finished, Timothy Williams took over our main story and I put together a sidebar offering analysis. Interestingly, the pollsters all predicted that voters wouldn't give a fig about the cancer, that they understood it was a highly treatable condition instead of a death sentence. But the political consultants I spoke with all looked for the deeper significance in why Giuliani had cast doubt on the likelihood of his continuing. Nelson Warfield, a former New Yorker and onetime press secretary to Bob Dole, unequivocally predicted, two hours after Giuliani had pronounced the words "I don't know," that he would drop out. Warfield told me he didn't think the mayor wanted to be senator anyway, and the cancer would allow him to get out of the race gracefully, without making it look as if he were slinking away from a fight.

Hillary was upstate that day. She steadfastly refused to make any prediction about how the mayor's illness might affect the race, saying only that she would pray for his speedy recovery. Minutes after Hillary's reaction hit the wire, the mayor's top City Hall press aide, tough-talking Sunny Mindel, called Timothy to complain that Hillary hadn't yet made a sympathy call to Giuliani. Timothy relayed the complaint to the Clinton camp, and two minutes later, Sunny called back to say that Hillary had just spoken to the mayor. It was one of the few conversations the two ever had. Later, Hillary's aides said she'd been trying to get through to City Hall all along but hadn't been able to reach him.

I led my sidebar that day like this: "Whether or not he remains in the race, Mayor Rudolph Giuliani's admission Thursday that he has prostate cancer has changed the dynamics of the U.S. Senate campaign in New York. Political experts predict that his fundraising will be hampered, rival Hillary Rodham Clinton will tone down her attacks and New Yorkers may change their views on Giuliani's candidacy. While some voters may feel sympathy toward a tough guy whose cancer suddenly makes him vulnerable, others could worry about his long-term health, or wonder if his refusal to commit to the campaign reveals a deeper ambivalence."

Because the news unfolded so early in the day, I actually made it out of the office in time to pick up my kids from school and make dinner.

That evening was one of the few nights I was planning to

go out. I belonged to a book club, and there was a meeting that night on my block. Because the book club meetings were just about the only thing that ever took me from home at night aside from the occasional Hillary event, they were somewhat sacred. I had a cellphone for work, but this was before the era when everyone carried their phone everywhere. So when my office started calling me at home that night to reach me about the Giuliani story, my husband didn't think it was worth going up the block to fetch me from the book club.

By the time I'd gotten home around 9:15 p.m., they'd called three times. It seemed one of Giuliani's campaign press aides, Juleanna Glover Weiss, didn't like my lead and had called my office asking that it be changed. She complained that it sounded as if Giuliani was going to drop out. The editor on duty was reluctant to change the story without checking with me, but she kept calling back, so the editor kept trying me at home. I was confident that my lead hadn't gone beyond what Giuliani himself had said, but it was clear from Juleanna's calls that the campaign staff was very worried about their future. I told the desk to call her back and offer to insert any comment that she wanted to make, but not to change the lead. I wanted to be fair and reflect their point of view, but they certainly weren't calling the shots on my story.

The mayor's campaign was run very differently from Hillary's. Her offices on Seventh Avenue just north of Macy's and Madison Square Garden were cramped and incredibly hectic; the tiny room that you walked into when you opened the door was plastered with an ever-changing exhibit of blown-up photos of Hillary in various poses on the campaign trail: Hillary holding a baby, Hillary talking to black women, Hillary meeting old people. It was like the anteroom for some sort of religious cult worshipping a blond lady with blue eyes and a big smile whose holy garments consisted of black pantsuits. The press staff worked out of an impossibly small room that just barely fit their desks and a TV. In contrast, Giuliani's campaign offices, downtown just a few blocks from City Hall, were spacious and open. The walls at Giuliani Central were mostly bare.

No photo lovefest here, just one outstanding feature: a digital neon clock that counted down the minutes to Election Day, with the red numbers for seconds changing so fast that they were just a blur.

Giuliani had said he would take a week or two to decide on a course of treatment for his cancer and that the implications of that would determine his political future. Between the day he divulged his cancer and the day he pulled out, "every tiny little Podunk press avail he had was packed with press and TV cameras from Japan to Sweden," our reporter Timothy Williams recalled. "It was bizarre, frustrating for the beat reporters, and he wouldn't tell us anything."

At one throwaway avail in Bryant Park to announce an annual celebration of Jewish heritage, the mayor showed up an hour late, surrounded by a half-dozen of his top advisers, to deliver another shocker: He was planning to separate from his wife, Donna Hanover.

"He seemed genuinely sad: muted, hurting, visibly pained," Timothy recalled. "It was very odd to see him like this. Usually he is quite loud. That day, he barely spoke above a whisper, which made the setting oddly intimate because the reporters that were there had to crowd around close to him to hear what he was saying. This is a guy who usually refused to answer the most innocuous personal question, and here he was laying himself bare before us."

When asked about the prospects for his Senate campaign, the mayor answered, "I'm not really thinking about politics right now." But it seemed to add evidence to the theory that he was leaning toward dropping out of the race.

Timothy asked Giuliani if he had told his wife that he was planning to make this announcement. "He kind of stuttered and ultimately said no," Timothy recalled. "They had discussed separation, but she didn't know he was going to go public."

Giuliani also used the press conference to confirm another rumor that had been kicking around: He had an ongoing relationship with another woman, Judi Nathan.

Just a few hours later, Donna Hanover summoned reporters to hear her side of it in a tearful, dramatic news conference outside Gracie Mansion, the mayor's residence.

"Today's turn of events brings me great sadness," she said. "I had hoped that we could keep this marriage together. For several years, it was difficult to participate in Rudy's public life because of his relationship with one staff member. Beginning last May, I made a major effort to bring us back together. Rudy and I re-established some of our personal intimacy through the fall. At that point he chose another path. Rudy and I will now discuss the possibility of a legal separation."

What a bombshell! The "staff member" Donna said her husband had had a "relationship" with was obviously Cristyne Lategano, Giuliani's former press secretary. Lategano had sold sneakers before volunteering on the mayor's 1993 campaign; she had managed to catch his eye and eventually got herself installed as his chief press aide, despite her lack of experience. An article in Vanity Fair eventually alleged what many local reporters suspected but had been unable to get any hard evidence for: that she and the mayor were romantically involved. She and Giuliani both vociferously denied the rumors, and she left the mayor's staff after six years and parlayed her City Hall connections into a job heading NYC & Co., a new name for the old Convention & Visitors Bureau. A short time later she married a freelance golf writer. In the days that followed Donna's dramatic press conference, Cristyne again denied that they'd been anything more than co-workers putting in long hours. And Giuliani, who had started to actually seem like a thoughtful, introspective guy after his cancer diagnosis, blew up at reporters who shouted questions about his philandering after Donna dropped her bomb.

"Don't you guys have the slightest bit of decency!" he barked to the City Hall press corps. "Shhhh! Do you realize you embarrass yourself doing this in the eyes of just about everybody?" To a questioner who asked about sleeping arrangements at Gracie Mansion, he shouted, "Oh, get out of here! Get lost, get lost, that's a sneaky way of trying to invade somebody's personal life."

Of course, everyone had known for years that the mayor's marriage was for show. The only real mystery was why he and Donna hadn't gotten divorced. Because both of them are Catholics with two school-age children, Andrew and Caroline, one school of thought was that they stayed together for faith and family. But there was a less charitable theory: that Donna wanted to stay in the marriage because being first lady of New York City provided her an instant publicity niche that she could use to further her acting ambitions. When she'd met Giuliani, he was the chief federal prosecutor for New York, crusading against mobsters and white-collar criminals; she was a local television news reporter. After he was elected, she continued her career. She became host of a cable show on the Food Network, she got good reviews for a supporting role in a movie and landed parts on soap operas, and she had been on the verge of appearing in a feminist-themed Broadway show called "The Vagina Monologues" when Giuliani's cancer was made public and she postponed her participation in the show.

Donna had not campaigned at all for her husband when he was running for re-election as mayor in 1997, and she was just as invisible during his Senate campaign. But there was one notable Donna sighting before Giuliani dropped out of the race. She and Hillary both received awards from the Women's Leadership Network, and for a few brief moments, they were in the same hotel ballroom at the same time.

Hillary sat on the dais from the beginning of the event until the end, while Donna magically appeared from behind a curtain when it was her turn to speak, made a self-congratulatory speech thanking New York for allowing her to prove that you could be a working mother and the city's first lady, and disappeared again behind the curtain. I'd expected a handshake, maybe even an air kiss, between the two of them. After all, they had so much in common: bad feelings toward Giuliani and sticking out marriages to philandering men. But as far as I could tell, they barely made eye contact.

As for Giuliani's new squeeze, he'd been parading Judi Nathan in public for several months before the media caught on that she was more than just some random supporter. She'd accompanied him to the St. Patrick's Day parade and the Inner Circle show, a spoof on city politics staged by reporters. But not until a few days before the prostate cancer revelation, as the mayor ostentatiously strolled around Manhattan with her while photographers snapped away, had it become obvious what was going on. But going public with Judi wasn't careless behavior; this was a social announcement from a guy whose sexual health and disintegrating marriage were about to become national topics of discussion.

Getting Hillary to comment on the news about Giuliani's marriage was even harder than getting her to comment on his cancer. It became a sort of game. Every time she spoke to the press during the three weeks between the time the mayor announced he had cancer and the day he dropped out of the race, we'd try a dozen different ways to get her to say something. How was it affecting her campaign? Wasn't it hard to continue campaigning with all this uncertainty, or, conversely, wasn't it easier to continue campaigning when the other side was imploding? Did she have any advice for the mayor? Who did she think would replace him? It didn't matter— she gave the same answer every time: "I'm just going to keep on doing what I've been doing all along, which is to keep focused on the issues." It was undoubtedly the right way to go, both politically and as a matter of good taste, not to mention as a woman who had survived a screwed-up marriage of her own. And the more she soldiered on, keeping her campaign commitments at fundraisers and union rallies and ladies' luncheons, the more respectable she looked in light of Giuliani's soap opera. In fact, rather than being unsettled by the chaos on the other side, she seemed, if anything, to be radiating a calm, sunny confidence.

But internally, the campaign was not looking forward to losing Giuliani as an opponent. "By the time Giuliani got out, we didn't want him to get out," one insider told me. "Hillary was very comfortable with Giuliani as her opponent. She knew who he was and how to deal with it."

And the mayor's lack of interest in upstate New York made the campaign feel increasingly secure. "Every time Giuliani said, 'Who cares about the Listening Tour?' he was basically saying to upstaters, 'I'm not going to listen,'" the Clinton campaign adviser added.

Finally, on Friday, May 19, 2000, just over three weeks after the mayor had made his cancer public, he announced his withdrawal from the race. The main reason, he said, was that he couldn't decide on a course of treatment with the simultaneous pressure of making a decision about the Senate race.

Rick Lazio, a Long Island congressman who looked younger than his 42 years, had seemed absurdly presumptuous when he'd declared an interest in running for the Senate months earlier, only to be ordered by Gov. George Pataki to get out of Giuliani's way.

But when Giuliani dropped out, it looked like Lazio was off to a fabulous start. He'd already quietly raised $5 million for a campaign nobody imagined he'd ever wage, and as a fresh-faced, likable, happily married suburban father with no political baggage, he was the perfect replacement for the mayor, whose cancer, messed-up marriage and acerbic personality added up to one big pile of negatives.

In fact, while Hillary had certainly had her share of screw-ups (the Suha kiss, the St. Patrick's Day controversy, the FALN flap) at least her mistakes only looked like the foolish blunders of a neophyte. The mayor's troubles, in contrast, looked egocentric and sometimes even heartless. He tried to shut down the Brooklyn Museum because he didn't like a painting of a black Madonna decorated with elephant dung and pictures of bare bottoms. He demonized a black man, Patrick Dorismond, who was fatally shot in a confrontation with police, by saying that Dorismond had a "propensity to violence" and allowing the release of Dorismond's sealed juvenile record for a robbery arrest at age 13. And he ordered police to take any homeless person found sleeping in a public place to a shelter; those who refused to go would be given a summons or arrested. "Streets do not exist in civilized cities for the purpose of sleeping there. Bedrooms are for sleeping," the mayor declared. I wondered whether Giuliani was aware of a slightly different declaration by 19th-century essayist Anatole France: "The law, in its majestic equality, forbids the rich as well as the poor to sleep under bridges, to beg in the streets and to steal bread."

The mayor had also been involved in nearly two dozen lawsuits contending he had violated the First Amendment by closing City Hall Plaza to the public and denying permits for various demonstrations. He'd lost nearly every case. All of these controversies made it easy for the Clinton campaign to deflect criticism of her missteps by picking on his.

The mayor's personality was also a good issue for Hillary's people to focus on because, in truth, she and Giuliani did not much disagree on a lot of the real issues that normally divide Democrats and Republicans.

But all that changed once Lazio entered the race. Lazio's views, while hardly right-wing, were much more conservative than Giuliani's: He opposed mandatory gun licensing, late-term abortion, Medicaid-funded abortions and civil unions for gay couples. Republicans, meanwhile, were thrilled to finally have, in Lazio, a candidate who was actually willing to campaign outside the five boroughs. By the end of his first 48 hours in the race, Lazio had visited nearly as many upstate cities as Giuliani had during the previous three months.

Giuliani made his big announcement about dropping out of the race on a Friday, which was my usual day off. It was the day I kept my younger son home from day care, picked up my older son at 3 p.m. instead of sending him to after-school, went to the library and hung out in the playground, just as I imagined stay-at-home moms doing. My husband called me midday to give me a heads-up that Giuliani was going to make the big announcement that afternoon, but my boss was nice enough not to call me in. I thought about volunteering to help out with the coverage, but I knew Hillary's news conference was already in the capable hands of someone else from my office, and I decided that, for a change, I'd pick the kids over Hillary and get the details of the story from TV news and the papers, just like everybody else. Danny had a playdate that afternoon with a friend, and I didn't want to let him down. I bought the kids ice cream after school from a Mister Softee truck, and by the time we got home, Lazio had scheduled a press conference for the next morning to launch his own campaign.

CHAPTER 8

Hillary Woos the Jews

The photo of Hillary kissing Palestinian leader Yasser Arafat's wife, Suha, on a visit to the Middle East dogged her throughout her Senate campaign. But there was another brief bubble that could have been even more damaging around an allegation that Hillary had used an anti-Semitic slur. Lucky for Hillary, the accuser was one of those people the Clintons had known in Arkansas who would occasionally pop out of the woodwork with a bizarre story of one sort or another. From the media's point of view, the best part of this debacle was that Hillary invited us to her house in Westchester for a press conference where she denied the allegation. We didn't get to go inside but it was as close as any of us ever came to the Clintons' New York home. Even better, her denial of the accusation ended in a moment where it seemed like the curtain on her emotions had actually lifted. We were sure we'd all seen a tear! Alas, if there was a tear, the photos didn't capture it. Once again, Hillary managed to keep a lid on it.

• • •

It was a slow Sunday afternoon in July of 2000. I was sitting in the newsroom reading the thick weekend papers. The only news out there was an accusation from a new book alleging that Hillary called someone a "fucking Jew bastard" in 1974 in Arkansas. But while the New York Post and the Daily News had stories about what the press corps came to refer to as "FJB," the networks, The New York Times, Newsday and the AP were holding off reporting it. The accuser, Paul Fray, who worked on Bill Clinton's congressional campaign, was quoted in the book, "State of a Union," as saying that Hillary called him an FJB the night Bill lost that race. Weirdly, Fray was a Baptist, although he apparently had one Jewish grandparent. And he was not returning our phone calls.

Then I got a call in the newsroom from Hillary's aide Karen Dunn.

"Hey, Karen! What's up?" I figured she was calling to let me know when they were releasing the summaries for Hillary's campaign financial filings.

"We're holding a news conference," she said. "At Hillary's house. In Chappaqua. Fifteen Old House Lane."

"You're holding a news conference?" I repeated stupidly. "At Hillary's house?" I was certain I heard her wrong.

"Yup." She added that it was going to be at 3 p.m.

It was 1:20 p.m. The campaign office was in midtown Manhattan. Chappaqua was a 40-minute drive.

"How are you getting there?" I asked, figuring that if they were going up to Westchester in a cab, I could go with them.

"I'm not sure. We might try to get a van together."

Yeah, right. I'd waited for vans at Clinton campaign headquarters that never showed up, and I'd been on campaign vans that got lost or were driven by lunatics. I didn't have time for that, not with just an hour and a half to get to Chappaqua.

"Never mind, I'll figure it out on my own somehow. I assume this is about the book?"

"Yes."

"OK, we'll be there. Hey, listen, I know you're not really focused on this right now, but what's happening with the financial filings?"

"I see you have a story out on the wire saying we'll have them today, but we won't."

"Fine, see ya."

I hung up and started typing furiously. "Add to the Sunday Day Schedule. 3 p.m. Hillary Rodham Clinton holds news conference regarding allegation in new book; 15 Old House Lane, Chappaqua."

"I got news," I called out to the editor.

"Yeah?" She looked up.

"Hillary's holding a news conference. At her house. About the book."

Everyone in the newsroom looked at me like I was out of my mind.

"I'm going to move this day schedule item," I said, typing the commands to send it out on the AP local wire to every newspaper and radio and TV station in the metropolitan area. Then I started typing a lead for the digest, which is a preview of the top stories we're working on that gets sent out on the wire each afternoon.

"CHAPPAQUA, N.Y. - Hillary Rodham Clinton holds a news conference at her Westchester home to respond to allegations contained in a new book that she used an anti-Semitic obscenity in 1974. Slug: NY Senate-Clinton. By Beth J. Harpaz. Associated Press Writer."

I stored the lead in my computer, told the editor the file name, and started dialing for Metro-North, the commuter train that runs from Manhattan to Westchester. I could make a train from Grand Central, arriving just in time.

Meanwhile Suzanne Plunkett, an AP photographer on desk duty for the day, was trying to get my attention to make sure she heard me right, that there was a press conference at Hillary's house. She made a few phone calls to rustle up a photographer, but after striking out, decided she should go herself. "Let me see if I can get somebody else to run the desk here and I'll drive you up," she said.

"Don't bother. There's a train in 15 minutes. I can make it."

I typed another message for the national editors, letting them know the financial filings wouldn't be released that day. Then I threw a notebook and tape recorder in my bag and ran out the door.

When I arrived at Grand Central, somebody ahead of me at the information booth was asking for very complicated directions to Little Italy, and the clerk was telling her the wrong train to take. Ordinarily I would have butted in like a good New Yorker and straightened them both out, but now I was desperately rushing to make this train. Two minutes to go.

Finally the woman left and I got my track number. I ran

downstairs, jumped on the train, and sat down. I bought my ticket from a conductor and put my head back.

Suddenly I was in a panic. This couldn't be right. I must have misunderstood Karen. Hillary couldn't possibly be holding a press conference about this. There's no way she would dignify this kind of accusation by talking to us about it. And she couldn't possibly be doing it at her house. The only time she'd ever talked to anybody at her house was when she and the president moved in, and the press was camped out in their cul-de-sac. She was way too private and paranoid to actually invite us there. And it couldn't possibly be happening on such short notice. Sure, the Clinton campaign made a lot of last-minute schedule changes, but not like this.

In my head, I went over my conversation with Karen. Did I somehow misunderstand? Checklist: She definitely told me this was about the book. She definitely gave me Hillary's address. She definitely said 3 p.m.

We were at Valhalla. Did I miss my stop? I strained to hear the announcements and looked around. Any other time I'd covered Hillary in Westchester or Long Island, I'd run into other reporters on the train. I didn't see any familiar faces. Suddenly we were in Chappaqua. I got off the train. I had to go to the bathroom, but there was no time.

I got in a cab and gave the driver the address. He turned around and smiled.

"My cousin lives on Old House Lane," he said knowingly.

"Yeah?"

"Whenever the Clintons are there, they have the dogs sniff the school bus for bombs."

"Really?"

"And my cousin invited the Secret Service agents over for a barbecue one day, but they never came." The driver was clearly miffed by this.

We turned off a two-lane road onto a tree-lined side street. I saw other reporters and Secret Service agents milling about. I paid and got out. I saw one of the advance guys, Steve Feder.

"Steve," I said. "I really have to go to the bathroom."

"Sorry. No way."

"I promise not to look in the medicine cabinet."

He shook his head.

"Isn't there a Secret Service bathroom I could use outside the house?"

"Nope."

"Geez, the least you could do is set up a port-a-potty in the woods for reporters."

I threw my bag down in the pile of cameras, tape recorders and knapsacks that had to be "swept," as the agents say, for bombs. One guy with a wire coming out of his ear knelt down and started turning on our cellphones one by one to make sure they weren't explosive devices. Another agent came over and asked me, "Have you been magged?"

That's short for magnetometer, a handheld scanner they use to detect metal objects. I held my arms up and the agent waved the device up and down my body.

I saw our photographer, Suzanne. "You made it!"

She smiled. "I can give you a ride back."

"Great."

A car drove up with US CONGRESS plates. Inside was U.S. Rep. Nita Lowey, the Jewish Westchester Democrat who would have run for the Senate seat if Hillary hadn't. From where we stood, you could barely see the whitewashed wooden shingles of the house beyond a narrow, wooded path. A gate blocking access to the path opened and Lowey's car drove in.

"Why is Nita Lowey here?" someone asked.

"Some of her best friends are Jewish, I guess," the answer came.

Then another car drove up. Howard Wolfson got out, and so did Adam Nagourney from the Times.

Gregg Birnbaum from the New York Post, who had just come from covering Lazio at an Irish festival, was there, too. He said Lazio absolutely refused to comment on FJB.

"I blocked his path to his van door and told him, 'I'm not letting you out of here till you say something about it,' but he wouldn't do it," Gregg said.

Next Liz Moore from Newsday arrived. She was one of the only other reporters on this gig who, like me, had kids. "I was having a family barbecue when I got the call for this," she said. "My 6-year-old doesn't get it."

"I know what you mean," I say. "My kids think I spend all this time with her because we're related. Aunt Hillary."

We started talking about what to ask her. Nobody said whether we believed the allegation or not. Our personal opinions were almost irrelevant. The only thing that mattered was the material we had available for our stories: quotes, photos, background and facts. Personally, I didn't think Hillary was capable of using that kind of language; she's too uptight. But every time I mentally tried to sort out the evidence, or lack thereof, in my head I saw President Clinton on national TV, talking about Monica Lewinsky while wagging his finger: "Ah did not have sexual relations with that woman!" I reminded myself that I believed him, too.

We were each given a copy of a two-page document written in cramped, nearly illegible cursive. After a moment we realized that this is a letter to Hillary from Paul Fray, the man who accused Hillary of calling him an FJB. But the handwriting in the letter was so bad that as we tried to decipher it, we began reading it aloud, with each of us picking up the recitation when somebody else couldn't make out a word.

"This is like a seder," Adam muttered.

"Except that instead of there being four questions, there are 4,000," I added.

The letter was bizarre. Fray was begging Hillary's forgiveness for "things I said against you ... without factual foundation," declaring that he was living in squalor, asking her to come and read to his grandson. It was dated July 1997.

"Isn't it great that she could find this letter on five minutes' notice but she couldn't find the law firm files?" someone said, referring to files from the Arkansas firm she worked for that were related to the Whitewater scandal. Copies of the files mysteriously turned up at the White House after a two-year search.

A couple of TV crews arrived, and we went through the gate down the narrow path to the house we'd glimpsed through the trees. I wondered if maybe they were going to let us in the house. I mean, why else would she have summoned us all up here if not to let us inside?

We ended up on a lush lawn by the side of the house. A simple perennial garden grew a few feet away, with orange daylilies and purple coneflowers, very understated and wild-looking. A weather-beaten white wicker couch with a faded floral pillow seat was the only object in the garden. I'd imagined Hillary's taste ran more to fussy French cast-iron benches.

This was my first look at the house. It was surrounded by big trees and positioned on the property in such a way that you couldn't see the whole thing from where we stood. Impossible to tell how big it was or discern the layout, or even tell where the doors were. It didn't look all that fancy; I'd certainly seen more imposing homes in Westchester.

One of the cameramen started filming a background shot of the yard and the house. Karen Finney, tall Karen as opposed to Karen Dunn, who was short Karen, put her hand on the cameraman's shoulder and shook her head. Before the campaign, Finney worked in Washington as a press aide in the first lady's office, and she tended to be the most protective of Hillary of all the campaign staffers. I actually considered it a game to find a way around whatever Finney was trying to shut down. If she said no avail, what I loved more than anything was to stake Hillary out and get a question in. If Finney said not to interview someone who's part of the first lady's entourage, I made it my business to walk halfway around the building and find another entrance that put me right next to the person I wanted to talk to.

I didn't take her limit-setting too seriously, and she didn't take my hurdle-jumping personally. She did her job, and I did mine. Right then, for example, she thought she was being prudent by stopping a cameraman from shooting the house, while I thought it ridiculous that they dragged us up here for this and then wouldn't let us take pictures. As if some terrorist was going to figure out how to bomb this place because there was a shot of the shingles for five seconds on the 11 p.m. news.

"Anybody know what kind of house this is?" I asked. I grew up in Manhattan, and suburban house types are beyond my frame of reference. I knew we'd reported it in previous stories about the Clintons purchasing the house, but now I couldn't remember the right term. "Ranch, cape, colonial?"

"I think it's a Dutch colonial," Liz said. "And are those peony bushes over there?"

"Peony season is over," I said.

"I know, but I think those are the bushes without the flowers."

I shrugged. We were all scribbling these little details down in our notebooks.

Now it was clear that we were not going to be allowed inside. The TV crews were setting up in a semicircle, so the house would be behind Hillary and in their shot when she comes out. Newspaper photographers crouched on the ground in front of the camera crews. Did I want to be on her right, where Adam and Gregg were sitting on the wet grass, to get better sound on my tape recorder, or did I want to be straight ahead of her, so if I asked a question, she couldn't ignore me? I opted for straight ahead.

"Heads up!" someone called. We turned on our tape recorders.

Here she came, with Lowey by her side. Oddly, they both wore cream-colored pantsuits. Accidental or coordinated? I reminded myself that with the Clintons, nothing is accidental.

Lowey started by expressing her outrage that anybody could think Hillary was capable of saying such a thing. I wondered what she was saying about Hillary back when the first lady big-footed her out of the Senate race. Then it was Hillary's turn. She said she called us here to state unequivocally that she never made this remark. Her eyes were puffy and she looked exhausted.

Then she started answering questions. No, she didn't recall

being in the room with Fray when he said she made the remark. I thought to myself: It never sounds good to hear a Clinton say "I don't recall."

No, she never responded to the letter that was handed out, but she was releasing it to us to prove that the people accusing her of this had no credibility.

She started looking around. This news conference was almost over and I still didn't understand why we were there. My turn to jump in.

"Mrs. Clinton," I called out. "Are you aware that a lot of news organizations, including my own and many others represented here today, had not planned to do a story on this because of the questionable nature of the material? Your being here guarantees that this is news for all of us. Why are you doing this?"

This was a somewhat self-serving question. I was basically pointing out that the AP, the Times, and Newsday, not to mention the networks, hadn't joined the tabloids in running a story that could not be confirmed by anybody except the sole guy making the accusation. Was I ass-kissing? A close call. But I really, really didn't understand why she was doing this press conference. And I really, really wanted her to know that whatever headlines her statements generated, on the wire or anywhere else, were her doing, not ours.

"You know, Beth," she began. It's stupid, but it was always a thrill when she used my name. And no doubt she realized how ingratiating it was, which is why politicians always try to use first names when talking to people. When I used to tell non-journalists I was covering her campaign, they'd often ask, "But does she know you?" It was only after she started answering my questions by using my first name that I could confidently respond, "Yeah, she knows me."

She went on to say that she'd been accused of a lot of things over the past eight years, "including complicity to murder," a reference to the suicide of White House aide Vince Foster, and that she had a policy of ignoring most of the allegations. But she said she couldn't ignore this one and decided to hold a press conference so that "anyone who tries to get someone else to believe this will at least have to say, 'Well, she says it's not true.'"

All of a sudden she brought the side of one hand down with a chop into the palm of her other hand for emphasis and raised her voice.

"You're darn right it's not true!" she said, for the first time sounding really angry and upset after 15 minutes of emotionless denials. "It's absolutely false! I'm just sick and tired of this kind of politics."

I realized Peter Moses, a producer for Channel 9 news, had squeezed himself next to me so that he was directly in front of her, too. Peter was the ultimate "How do you feel?" TV guy, the kind of person who doesn't mind sticking his mic in the face of someone who's crying to try to get a quote. Watching him do this sort of thing made me glad I don't work for TV. On the other hand, I had to admit, I kind of admired it.

He had that impish look on his face that meant he was about to pounce. He grinned naughtily and called out in a singsong tone of voice to Hillary, "But why aren't you angrier?" There was a low groan from a couple of the other reporters.

Months later, when I asked Peter about this particular incident, he told me he'd gotten "a lot of grief" from some of the other reporters who accused him of trying to make her cry. "I just wanted to see if there was any real emotion under the veneer," he said. And personally, I didn't have a problem with him doing it. I was just glad it wasn't me who asked it.

His question elicited a glare from Hillary. "I am angry. I'm very angry. But you know…"

Now her voice started to break and she looked away from us for a moment. She was about to cry! Hillary the Ice Queen was letting us see her inner feelings! She wouldn't let us in her house. That would be asking too much. We could never sit with her in her van or hang out and chat the way we do with other candidates. But she had invited us onto her property and let us come as close as she possibly could, physically and emotionally. Her eyes were now welling up. This was amazing! Hillary was going to shed a tear! I didn't know whether to feel sorry for her or happy for me, because this was news.

Then she swallowed. The sob, however close it might have come to spilling out, was gone. Back to the cerebral first lady who never showed her real feelings. "Her Majesty's a pretty nice girl, someday I'm gonna make her mine," the Beatles once sang, and sometimes that's how I felt about Hillary at those rare times when she seemed to be lifting the curtain and letting us in on her inner feelings. It's what all journalists want to do to the people they're interviewing: get inside their heads.

But I knew I wouldn't be making Hillary mine that day, once the sob was gone.

"I learned a long time ago that the people who generate this kind of stuff are really hoping to divert attention from what's important in a campaign..." she began. Yeah yeah yeah. The press conference was over.

I saw our photographer, Suzanne. "Wow!" she said. "I think we saw a tear."

"Really?" I said.

A Daily News reporter came over. "A tear? You sure? You gonna look at your film now?"

Our photographers all used digital film and could edit and transmit their pictures onto the AP wire by satellite computers from anywhere—a war zone, a highway, anywhere. But Suzanne had left the computer in the office that day and wanted to get back. And we were still years away from the era when you could take a picture on a cellphone and make it public online in a matter of seconds.

I still had to go to the bathroom. I saw Howard and begged him to let me use the Secret Service facilities.

"I'll see what I can do." That was his response to everything. I could see it wasn't going to get me a bathroom that day.

I walked back with Suzanne to her car. Everybody had been forced to park a quarter mile down the road. "You still need a bathroom?" she asked.

"Nah." Now I just wanted to get back. I replayed my tape, transcribed the quotes, pulled out my cellphone and started dictating to a reporter back at the office, a "rewrite," as in the old newsroom movie scenes where a hard-bitten cop reporter in a fedora picks up the phone and says, "Hello, sweetheart? Get me rewrite."

By the time we reached the office, the story was nearly ready to move on the wire. Somebody had grabbed a quote off CNN from the author of the book, Jerry Oppenheimer, and a fax had come in with a statement from President Clinton. I threw a little into the story from each of those, tinkered with the lead and handed it to the desk. Eight-hundred words and no room for the Dutch colonial, peony bushes or the purple coneflowers. Too bad.

I walked over to where Suzanne and an editor were looking at a couple of photos up on a computer screen. Hillary looked mean in one, mad and tired in another and puffy-eyed and resigned in a third.

"No tears?" I asked.

"No tears."

I still needed to use the bathroom. Now that the story was done, I could.

The next day it occurred to me that Hillary was consciously portraying herself as a victim here, a victim of one of the many people who knew Bill and Hil back in Arkansas and who periodically grabbed the media's attention with an allegation about something they did years before they were in the White House.

Now why would Hillary want us to view her as a victim? Because the last time everybody felt sorry for her, during the Monica Lewinsky scandal, her poll numbers were sky-high. It was a dynamic we would see play out at other moments as well. She got high marks from voters after a debate with her eventual Republican opponent, Rick Lazio, during which he approached her on the stage in what seemed to be a confrontational manner. More famous was the moment in New Hampshire during the 2008 presidential campaign when she seemed to choke back a tear answering a seemingly innocuous question about how she managed to pull herself together every day. She went on to win the primary.

The next time I saw Hillary after the news conference in Chappaqua, she was addressing a group from the New York Academy of Sciences. As usual, her intellectual mastery was impressive: She chatted knowledgeably about the human genome—one of her favorite nerd topics—and high-speed Internet connections and medical research and technology-based economic development. None of us understood any of it, but it seemed to go over big with this audience of engineers, researchers, professors and high-tech financiers. Of course, there wouldn't be any news from this; we were just here in case she said anything else about FJB. I sat next to Bob Hardt, who covered the race with Gregg Birnbaum for the Post. Bob liked to say that the two of them were like Laurel and Hardy. Bob was bald, round, droll and deliberate and wore seersucker suits with a straw hat; while Gregg, wiry and hyper with a brown beard, favored dark sunglasses and had a large collection of blazers, my favorite being a herringbone number the color of gourmet mustard. Both of them were savvy and smart and had saved my ass on any number of occasions with quotes I missed or background I didn't have.

On that particular day, Bob was playing with the newest toy to make the rounds of journalists: a Palm Pilot. In "The Boys on the Bus," reporters covering the Nixon-McGovern race shared tape recorders, filed their stories via Western Union telegrams and flung TV film into helicopters to get it back to their stations in time for the next broadcast. In the 2000 Senate race, everybody had his or her own beeper, cellphone and tape recorder; TV crews transmitted live via satellite; and there was no sound in this world as comforting to me as the clack-clack-clack of Adam Nagourney typing away on his laptop during a Hillary news conference. One day as I sat next to Adam on a campaign van, he even plugged his laptop into his cellphone and sat there reading his email as if it were no big deal. A few years into the future, we'd all be getting our emails on our phones, filing our stories digitally from the scene and sending photos in with the touch of a button. But at the turn of the century, just getting an email in a moving car seemed miraculous.

Then Bob used the tiny pointer on his device to see what was in that day's Washington Post—another revelation in that era, looking at news online. "Hey, they used your story on the Chappaqua news conference," he told me. It was the first time I'd seen one of my stories on a mobile device.

Our next Hillary event was on Ellis Island and it involved a lot of waiting. Liz Moore from Newsday helped me pass the time by telling me her nanny horror stories, like the one who had her boyfriend half-living in Liz's house and the other one who kept crashing Liz's car. Somebody asked me if I thought Hillary was making us wait on purpose. I didn't think she was doing it deliberately to piss everybody off; I thought she probably had people to meet, and a lunch to eat, and autographs to sign, and, well, if we all ended up standing in the hot sun for one or two or three hours, so what? Finally, around 3 p.m., we got our avail. The day's spin was all about Hillary proclaiming herself a victim and snidely suggesting that FJB was part of a larger Republican plot against her. Of course, there was no evidence to suggest that FJB had anything to do with the GOP; I'd called the author of the book where the allegation surfaced and he told me himself that he was a Democrat who voted for the Clintons. The guy who made the accusation, Paul Fray, was one of Bill Clinton's campaign workers.

When I got back to my desk, I found that the quote of the day came not from Hillary but from Lazio, who'd changed his "no comment" on FJB to an "I don't know what to believe." I also called Gail Sheehy, who'd interviewed Fray for the biography she'd written the year before, "Hillary's Choice." She told me Fray's wife had told her the FJB story but she'd left it out of her book because she didn't believe it.

I spent the next day working on a story about Fray. I'd read somewhere that Fray had been disbarred, but when I called the Arkansas State Supreme Court to get the records, they claimed the reasons for the revocation weren't public information. So I asked one of AP's news researchers, Rhonda Shafner, to see what she could find, and within the hour she'd obtained the records through an Internet-based research service. The Arkansas Supreme Court Committee on Professional Conduct revoked Fray's license because, in 1977, he made a false entry on a court docket to change a DWI conviction for one of his clients to a dismissal. When he applied to have his license reinstated, he gave as evidence of his good moral character the fact that he'd obtained a master's degree from a Baptist divinity school. The judges denied the reinstatement of his license, but in their written opinions, they noted that Fray had suffered a brain hemorrhage a month after making the false entry in the court docket, and that he behaved in a "bizarre" and "forgetful" manner "before and after" the hemorrhage. Some of this behavior, the judges wrote, was caused in part by medication to which Fray had become addicted, although they noted that he later went into rehab. None of that was in the book containing the FJB allegation. But it all reminded me that conveying the truth in any story has as much to do with what you leave out as what you put in.

Gregg Birnbaum, meanwhile, arranged for Fray to take a lie detector test and reported the results in the Post. "There's no doubt in my mind that Mr. Fray is truthful," the polygrapher who administered the exam in Arkansas told Gregg, even though another polygraph expert deemed the results "inconclusive." Fray also told Gregg that despite the controversy over FJB, he hoped Hillary would win. "She will make an excellent senator," he said.

Over the next few days, the Camp David peace talks collapsed without any agreement. Arafat reiterated his threat to declare a unilateral Palestinian state, which the Clinton administration immediately condemned. Then Hillary issued her own statement in which she called for a withdrawal of all U.S. aid if the Palestinians took it upon themselves to declare statehood in the absence of a peace agreement. I checked all the stories we had on the Camp David talks; Hillary had definitely gone beyond her husband in advocating a cutoff on aid. That afternoon she had an appearance at a nursing home in Manhattan. I hoped we'd get a chance to ask her about it.

The nursing home event seemed endless. She showed up late, watched old people getting physical therapy, then made a speech to a group of nursing home residents and union members who work as attendants.

Karen Dunn came to the back of the room where the press was standing and told us we could ask questions when she was done talking.

It wasn't an ideal setting, as we were separated from her by an audience of 200 people, and her speech had been about issues related to the care of the elderly. "I have a question, but it's not about any of this," I whispered to Dunn. "That's OK," she assured me. "Go ahead and ask it."

A couple of reporters had wandered up to the front of the room and jumped in first with two questions about nursing home care. I looked at Dunn and she nodded at me. So I called out, from the back, a question about Hillary's stand ending U.S. aid to the Palestinians. "Are you going beyond your husband's policy in making this statement?"

"I may be, but it's what I believe," she replied.

Then another reporter asked her what she thought of the peace talks. She spent several minutes praising the Israeli prime minister. "What about Arafat?" Eileen Murphy of ABC called out.

All of a sudden there was an impatient murmur in the audience.

"Health care!" called out one lady.

"Yeah! We want to talk about health care!" shouted another.

Now the entire room was filled with cries of "Health care!" It looked as if the media were about to be run out of town by a bunch of old ladies in wheelchairs for daring to ask about the Israeli peace talks. We looked at each other, shook our heads and rolled our eyes. Hillary shrugged a little, smiling, as if to say, "See? This is what the people want from me." She could have said, "I'll just answer that last question and then we'll get back to health care." But she didn't. There were a few more questions and mini-speeches about health care, then it was over.

A few days later, Hillary said in a radio interview that the U.S.

embassy in Israel should immediately be moved to Jerusalem from its current location in Tel Aviv. Coincidentally, or more likely not so coincidentally, President Clinton was quoted in The New York Times that day saying that he would review the issue of moving the embassy before the end of the year. Again, Hillary was going a baby step further than Bill, almost making it look as if she were pushing the administration's policies.

The same day, at a synagogue appearance, Lazio accused Hillary of "flip-flopping" on the embassy relocation. Back in December, she'd said she did not support the immediate move of the embassy. The AP story had Lazio in the lead accusing Hillary of reversing her position. Karen Dunn called seven times to complain about that, saying Hillary's statement on the embassy should have been the lead, not Lazio's comment on it. But there was nothing wrong with the story, so we left it as is.

What the entire episode really showed was how much Jewish voters mattered in New York. Jewish turnout in those years was typically just 12 to 14 percent of the electorate, and Jewish Democrats outnumbered Jewish Republicans about 6 to 1. But a small group of several hundred thousand politically moderate Jews are considered swing voters. Most of the ultra-Orthodox typically vote Republican, although Hillary did manage to corner endorsements from a couple of Hasidic sects, and Lazio would never get the unshakably liberal Jews for whom pulling the GOP lever was anathema.

But the past few Senate races suggested that a Democrat who couldn't get more than 60 percent of the Jewish vote couldn't win. Mark Green and Robert Abrams, both Democrats who failed to beat Al D'Amato for Senate, did not reach the 60 percent mark. Both were liberal Jewish Democrats but both ran flawed campaigns. In contrast, Chuck Schumer, also a relatively liberal Jewish Democrat, had captured closer to 70 percent of the Jewish vote, and he had beaten D'Amato. Ironically, D'Amato's use of a Yiddish term had helped Schumer win. At a private meeting with Jewish leaders shortly before the 1998 election, D'Amato called Schumer a "putzhead." The word "putz" generally connotes a bumbling fool but literally means "penis." Someone who was at the meeting tattled on D'Amato, and Schumer accused him of using a "Yiddish slur." At first D'Amato denied it, but then Ed Koch and a few others who'd been at the meeting confirmed that D'Amato had said it, making him look not only like a liar but also like a pretty crude guy.

Schumer effectively used the incident to make the case to voters that D'Amato, who had a reputation for making outrageous comments and who'd been rebuked by the Senate Ethics Committee for allowing his brother's lobbying firm to use the senator's office to help a client, could simply not be trusted to tell the truth or to behave appropriately. D'Amato was popular in the Jewish community for taking on the Swiss banking industry over Holocaust reparations, but that wasn't enough to make up for "putzhead."

Polls showed Hillary's support among Jews at between 50 and 60 percent. That actually wasn't bad for a non-Jew with the FJB allegation and the Suha Arafat kiss in her carpetbag. But the conventional wisdom was that she'd have to do better than that to win the election, and that's what all these trips to synagogues, pronouncements on Israeli policies and phone calls from the campaign were about. (In the end, she got a little more than half the Jewish vote, about what she'd had all along, which led me to believe that her repeated attempts to portray herself as a great lover of all things Jewish, and her enemies' attempts to portray her as an anti-Semite, had canceled each other out.)

Hillary also had a way of getting herself in trouble on issues related to Israel. There was the comment she'd made back in 1998 that a Palestinian state was "very important" to the long-term prospects for peace in the Middle East. There was the Suha Arafat kiss. And then, in July, just four months before the election, there was the FJB allegation.

Shortly after the go-round over the location of the U.S. embassy in Israel, I ran into Frank Eltman, the AP reporter covering Lazio, at the office. We talked on the phone constantly, but since he was always out covering Lazio and I was always covering Hillary, we hardly ever saw each other. When we did, we couldn't stop chatting.

We were like two soldiers hanging out in a VFW hall or a couple of addicts in a 12-step program. It was as if nobody else in the world understood what we were going through. But this time Frank said he had something funny to tell me and motioned me over to where he was sitting. Then he started singing softly, to the tune of "Anything you can do, I can do better" from "Annie Get Your Gun":

Any Jew you can woo, I can woo better.
I can woo any Jew better than you.

I started laughing hysterically. This was simply the funniest campaign song I had ever heard. And the scene it conjured up from "Annie Get Your Gun" was perfect: Annie, or rather Hillary, and her male opponent in a sharpshooting contest, trying to outdo each other. The next time I covered Hillary, I sang it for everyone on the van, and we all agreed that it was not only hilarious, but also because it was a duet, it perfectly captured the dynamic between the candidates and the Jewish voters they were after.

Looking back on it after the election, it was so hard to pick out a favorite moment from the Jew-wooing effort. Was it the day Hillary held a press conference with Elie Wiesel, aka "my good friend Elie Wiesel," to express outrage over anti-Semitic statements from a textbook used by the Palestinian Authority? Needless to say, this was not a pressing issue in the New York Senate race.

Or maybe it was the day she went to a YWHA in the Bronx with Hadassah Lieberman, aka "my good friend Hadassah Lieberman," and said that she'd been to Israel five times. That event had been preceded by a speech to a meeting of the National Council of Jewish Women and a visit to a Hebrew day school on Long Island, prompting Joel Siegel of the Daily News to ask as we got back in the van, "Does anybody know how to say 'pander' in Yiddish?"

One of Hillary's Jewish events seems much more memorable in hindsight than it did at the time: her visit on Aug. 8, 2000, to New Square, a Hasidic village in Rockland County. Hillary met that day with the village's spiritual leader, Rabbi David Twersky. Despite disagreeing with her on the issue of vouchers to help families pay for private and parochial schools, Twersky endorsed Hillary's candidacy. As a result, on Election Day, Hillary got exactly 1,400 votes from the village, while Lazio got exactly 12.

The monolithic nature of the vote was not unusual; Hasidic voters typically follow their rabbis' lead. Even their support for a Democrat was not particularly noteworthy; this particular sect often flip-flopped between parties, supporting Bush for president in 1992, Clinton for president in 1996, D'Amato for Senate and Gore for president in 2000.

But New Square's support for Hillary became extremely newsworthy after the election, when Bill Clinton gave clemency to four men from the community.

The men had been convicted of ripping off millions of dollars in government grants for poor college students by establishing a phony school in Brooklyn; most of the money had been illegally funneled to real schools in New Square that were not eligible for government funding.

Bill Clinton commuted the men's sentences from more than five years in prison to less than three years after meeting with Twersky and a delegation from the village in the White House on Dec. 21, 2000, six weeks after his wife's victory. Hillary was present for the meeting, but later insisted, when asked about the appearance of a political payback, that the president had made the decision to grant the clemency without any input from her. "I had no opinion at the time," she said.

Bill Clinton's pardon of Marc Rich, who'd fled the United States to avoid prosecution for illegal oil deals with Iran, had a Jewish connection, too: Ehud Barak, then Israeli prime minister, had lobbied for it. It was ironic that Hillary had to fight accusations of anti-Semitism before she was elected because of the Suha kiss and the FJB scandal, because once she took office, she and her husband had to fight the perception that they'd done too many favors for the Jewish community.

Another memorable episode in Hillary's campaign for Jewish votes occurred when she visited a nursing home for Holocaust survivors with Tom Lantos, aka "my good friend Tom Lantos," a California Democrat who was the only Holocaust survivor to serve in Congress. Three weeks before the nursing home event, Lantos had told the New York Post about the existence of the photo that showed Lazio shaking hands with Yasser Arafat. The photograph was taken during a visit to the Middle East by a delegation that included the Clintons, Lantos, Lazio, and many other U.S. government officials. Lantos said he'd decided to tip the Post off to the picture because he was angry that Lazio had criticized the president for shaking Fidel Castro's hand during a United Nations gathering in New York. But the photo also made a nice comeback to people who'd criticized Hillary for kissing Suha Arafat. Lazio didn't just appear to be shaking Arafat's hand in the interests of avoiding an international incident; he had a grin on his face from ear to ear and looked, in his boyish way, really excited to be meeting a famous person.

But the incident from the nursing home event that lived on and on in campaign lore was when Hillary said Lantos had been "ka-velling about his grandchildren." Kvelling is a Yiddish word that means gushing with joy and pride, the opposite of kvetching. Hillary had used the word appropriately, but her pronunciation was all wrong. Kvell is properly pronounced as one syllable, with the KV blend taking no longer to say than the FL in flute, but Hillary could only say it improperly, as ka-vell.

I thought maybe she was taking her cue from Sally Field, who'd bantered with a Jewish union organizer in the movie "Norma Rae" by muttering, "Ka-vetch, ka-vetch, ka-vetch."

I later found out that the first lady had had a "My Fair Lady"-style coaching session with her Jewish staffers during a routine conference call, but it hadn't done much good. It had been her idea to use the word kvell, but she'd known she needed a lesson on how to say it. She'd impressed her Jewish aides with her pronunciation on a few other occasions, getting the guttural ch in chutzpah just right during one of the debates with Lazio, and casually, but correctly, using the word shul (Yiddish for synagogue) at an event at the White

House. From her point of view, using these words showed that she had a certain comfort level with Jewish culture and maybe even earned her a brownie point or two for trying to fit in.

But mastering the pronunciation of kvell right turned out to be a lost cause.

"Kvuh, kvuh, it's one syllable, can't you hear it?" the aides had told her.

"Ka-vuh, ka-vuh," she'd replied. "That's what I said!"

I had one notable evening covering the Lazio campaign's efforts to make inroads with Orthodox Jewish voters. Lazio was doing a tour of Orthodox events in Brooklyn, and when we got to the third event, a celebration of the harvest festival Sukkot, it turned out that women were not allowed inside. This was not an uncommon practice in the Orthodox Jewish community, which I'd covered for the AP for years. But in my experience, whoever was handling the press coverage always made arrangements beforehand to ensure access for female reporters, whether that meant cordoning off a small area where we could observe the proceedings without sitting among the men, or recruiting an Orthodox woman to explain to us what was going on so that we wouldn't miss anything, or even just having someone take our tape recorders inside and turn them on at the right time.

None of that happened here. The women in the press corps with Lazio that night were simply left standing outside on the sidewalk while the men in the press corps and Lazio's all-male staff followed their candidate inside. At the next event, the same thing happened. A camerawoman for NY1, the local all-news cable station, handed her video camera to a male producer for a different station and asked him to take it inside so she could at least have a little bit of footage.

I was furious by the time it was all over and we got back into the van. I asked Gregg Birnbaum if he had a cellphone number for Jonathan Greenspun, Lazio's adviser on Jewish affairs, so I could call to complain. But when I tried the number, I couldn't get through.

"What's the big deal?" Gregg said to me. "There was no news at any of these events."

What's the big deal? I couldn't believe he'd said that! I was momentarily speechless, just sputtering with anger. My fury boiled up to the point where I simply reached over the back of the seat in front of me to where Gregg was sitting and started punching him in the shoulder.

Eventually I found my voice, but I was so mad that I'm not even sure what I said, and Gregg said he couldn't remember either. All he knows is that I totally lost it. I know I was thinking, "How would you feel if you showed up at an event and were told the Times and the AP can come in but not the Post? ... This would never happen on Hillary's campaign! ... How dare they do this! ... And they didn't even say they were sorry .... I went to the Lubavitcher rebbe's gravesite with Benjamin Netanyahu and I got a front-row seat, but when I go with Lazio to Borough Park, I can't even get in the door!" and so on. Gregg's ultimate revenge was reminding me of this episode, which I had sort of blocked out of my mind, and getting me to record it here for posterity.

The night after my ill-fated visit to Brooklyn, one of Hillary's Jewish advisers, Matthew Hiltzik, went back to the very same neighborhood to meet with leaders from the Bobovs, one of the Hasidic groups whose Sukkot celebration Lazio had visited (and I had been kept out of). Ironically, it turned out that the route to a political endorsement from this group was not by dropping in on an all-male gathering as Lazio had done, but through a meeting with the chief rabbi's wife, known as the rebbetzin.

"She's the classic example of a bold, strong woman behind the man," Matthew said. He was given the honor of being part of a group escorting the rebbetzin to synagogue that night, and on the Saturday night before the election, Hillary was invited to come to Borough Park herself, for a 90-minute meeting with a group of Bobover men and women. Republicans with contacts in the community had pressured the rabbi's wife not to meet with Hillary, but the rebbetzin had done what she thought was right and gone ahead with the first lady meeting anyway.

Lazio, in his contact with the group, had stressed his support for vouchers, which Hillary opposes. But she was able to talk about other issues that were equally compelling, like housing, health care and jobs, and in the end, Hillary got the Bobov endorsement.

CHAPTER 9

Hillary's Favorite Color

Sometimes I'm asked what it's like to be part of the press corps covering a big campaign. Sure, there's competition, and people are working on exclusive stories or features away from the scrum. But so much of your time on a campaign is spent waiting around with the same group of reporters that camaraderie develops. You get to know the other people; often times you help each other out if someone missed a quote that everybody else has. And inevitably, a lot of inside jokes develop. You make up ridiculous songs, you compete to do the best imitation of the speeches the candidate has given so many times that you've memorized it, and you even play stupid games—like the one described here.

• • •

"Scalia or Thomas?" somebody was saying. "Come on, what do you say? Scalia or Thomas?"

"I'd do 'em both," a woman answered in a deadpan voice.

"Thomas," said someone else with a snicker. "Could be interesting."

I looked up from my breakfast. We were sitting in a diner in August 2000 on the second day of Hillary's three-day tour of Long Island, and I was feeling slightly bummed out. I had planned to finish three stories while she was out here, the first a straightforward piece about her campaigning on Lazio's home turf, the second a feature story about the political instincts of her daughter, Chelsea, who was campaigning with her, and the third, a fun, light feature story about the candidates' "favorites"—favorite junk food, favorite color, favorite book.

The first story wrote itself with no trouble yesterday, but here it was, not even 9 a.m. a day later, and my prospects for finishing the other two stories were already looking bleak. Yesterday Chelsea had come off like a totally political animal, thriving on the attention of the public and the press, but today she seemed bored and unenthusiastic. And Karen Finney, Hillary's press aide, who had promised yesterday to help me get the answers from Hillary for my favorites list, which I had requested a month earlier, had just informed me that she didn't have a chance to do anything on it yet.

I was on one side of the dining room at a big round table with a few other reporters and campaign workers, while Hillary, Chelsea and some of the locals ate and chatted at a different table on the other side of the room. The first lady and her daughter were eating fruit, but most of the reporters had ordered the most unhealthy breakfasts possible: runny eggs, white toast, sausage, bacon and of course, lots of coffee, since we all got up at dawn to watch Hillary greet early-morning commuters at a Long Island Rail Road station.

I tuned in to the conversation at the table and realized I had no idea what my colleagues were talking about.

"Scalia or Thomas? What does that mean?" I said. "Why are you talking about George W.'s favorite judges?" Hillary was always pointing out in her speeches that Bush was an admirer of the most anti-abortion judges on the Supreme Court. It was one of those sound bites that every reporter who covered her could intone, from memory, along with her.

"You have to have sex with one of these people: Scalia or Thomas," said one of the other reporters. "And death is not an option. So, like, Schumer or D'Amato?"

Groans. "Yuck!" No one made a pick. "OK, Koch or Giuliani?"

The offerings rapidly devolved. Next was a choice between two of Hillary's advisers, and then a choice between two of the TV reporters who were not with us.

"This game is totally bizarre," I said. "You realize that, right?"

It was explained to me that this was one of the many pastimes I had missed out on by staying home during Hillary's upstate trips, where she was on the road for up to a week at a time.

I was reminded of the "Scalia or Thomas" game 15 years later when CNN played a version of it on the air with South Carolina Sen. Lindsey Graham before he participated in one of the Republican presidential debates. Gawker referred to the incident as an act of "mutual desperation" for both CNN and Graham. The reporter was asking Graham to say who he would "date, marry or make disappear forever," if the choices were Hillary, Sarah Palin or Carly Fiorina. It was painful to watch, but eventually Graham was cornered into saying that he'd date Palin, marry Fiorina and make Clinton disappear. (The actual game CNN had cleaned up for the air is "Fuck, marry or kill," not "date, marry or disappear.")

I don't think we'd ever have dreamed of trying to get one of the candidates to play these games back in 2000. But there was so much downtime and so little news that it wasn't unusual to find stuff like that happening on the press van. I had also learned how to play Punchy Bug, in which you punch the shoulder of the person sitting next to you in the press van every time you see a Volkswagen. And I had been taught a new song to the tune of "Someone's in the kitchen with Dinah":

> *Someone's in the Senate with Schumer*
> *Someone's in the Senate I know*
> *Someone's in the Senate with Schumer*
> *Strummin' on the old banjo*
> *And singin' H, I, LL-A-R-Y. H, I, LL-A-R-Y-I-I-I...*

This ditty was usually performed in an operatic basso, just as, I was told, it was first sung to Hillary and the press corps by a lounge singer named Spiro during a minor league baseball game in Jamestown. Since then, of course, my colleagues had improved upon it with such intelligent variations as "Someone's in the shower with Schumer." I added this lovely selection to the ever-growing repertoire in my brain that already included "Any Jew you can woo,

I can woo better" and "What if Hil were one of us? Could she tawk like one of us?"

As we followed Hillary and Chelsea out of the restaurant to the waiting vans, I checked out their dirty plates. I'd been slightly dubious of Finney's report that they were eating fruit, especially when we were all feasting on cholesterol and fat, but there were indeed leftover blueberries in bowls where they'd been sitting. We were forever writing details like this down in our notebooks, but at the end of the day there was hardly ever any room for it in our copy.

"By the way," said Finney with a smile, "in case you're wondering, yes, Hillary paid for their breakfast, and, yes, she left a tip." Hillary's tips had been an issue ever since the Washington Times made a headline out of her staff's failure to leave one for a waitress in an upstate restaurant where the first lady had been given a complimentary meal. The embarrassed campaign later mailed a savings bond to the waitress, a single mother.

Next stop after the diner was a day camp. Chelsea sat at a wood sculpture table with a bunch of little girls and absentmindedly made a tall pile of wood shapes. Then she wandered over to the pool where her mother was watching a relay race. But when Liz Moore of Newsday good-naturedly asked her if she thought the kids would vote for her mother, Chelsea stared straight ahead and walked away as if some terrible line had been crossed.

Chelsea had been friendlier a few weeks earlier when she'd accompanied her mother to a press conference on the steps of City Hall, her first appearance on the campaign trail in nearly a year. I'd asked Hillary during the Q-and-A if Chelsea was going to be showing up regularly from now on, and she'd said that was entirely up to Chelsea. When the event was over, we all ran over to where Chelsea was standing to see if she'd elaborate. Finney introduced us and we shook hands, but when I started to ask Chelsea whether we'd be seeing a lot of her in the future, Finney physically inserted herself between us, saying firmly, "Now, Beth, I think her mother answered that already."

"Hey, I'm a mom, I understand these things, and I think I heard her mother say that what Chelsea does is up to her," I said.

Chelsea perked up immediately. "You have children? How old are they?"

"Seven and 2, and they know all about your mother," I said with a smile. "They can pick her picture out of a photograph with a hundred other people in it."

"They're smarties," Chelsea said sweetly, then turned to head off with her mother's entourage.

Suddenly I felt like a dope. I'd wasted the two-minute window I'd had with Chelsea by talking about me. I'd rather talk about my kids than just about anything else, and Chelsea had been savvy enough to figure that out. One of the most basic rules of journalism is that when your source starts asking about you, you have to turn the conversation back to them. I hadn't done that, and now it was too late.

"Sorry about that, Beth," said Karen. "I just didn't want it to degenerate into a whole avail."

"Yeah, yeah. You do your job, I'll do mine," I said, feeling that I hadn't done it very well at all. The whole notion that Chelsea could come to a press conference and not take questions was infuriating enough. If she wanted to be private, fine, but don't stand 5 feet away from a pack of reporters and then let a campaign staffer protect you from the media. Soon after that, the White House announced that Chelsea planned to take off the fall semester of her senior year at Stanford to campaign with her mother and spend time with her father during his last months in office. I took Hillary at her word that this was Chelsea's decision, but it certainly didn't hurt the first lady to have her daughter along. And it didn't hurt Hillary's presidential campaign, 15 years later, when Chelsea had a child of her own, for Hillary to mention repeatedly that she was now a grandmother. Chelsea announced her second pregnancy during the 2016 campaign as well.

But back in 2000, we assumed that part of what brought Chelsea into the campaign was Lazio's two adorable little girls. "Vote for my dad!" they'd shout as the photographers snapped away. One day, when Lazio was being interviewed on ABC's "This Week," I sat in a TV studio with his wife, Pat, and the girls, waiting for his segment to start. Molly and Kelsey were like two little kittens, tumbling over each other in the hallway, using a rubber band they had found to play cat's cradle, hiding under the buffet, nibbling at the food, and then handing their dad a handful of crumbs when he came in the room. And Pat seemed like such a nice, normal person. I was shocked at being allowed to sit in a room with her and her kids. I couldn't imagine anything like this happening on the Hillary campaign.

Sit in a room with Chelsea and watch her mother on TV? Have a normal conversation with someone who's related to Hillary? Not have your bags searched and your movements restricted when you walk in the door? No way.

It also occurred to me that Chelsea could never be in her own little world the way the Lazio girls were, oblivious to all the busy grown-ups around them. Chelsea was always on when she was out with her parents, on display as the only child of important people, and instead of having a sibling to giggle with, her confidants were the people who'd been hired to protect her and make sure her needs were met. It was more like watching a princess venturing out among the common people than Take Your Daughter to Work Day.

Which isn't to say Chelsea didn't act as though she loved it. On the first day of the Long Island tour, at an outdoor rally in Great Neck, the 20-year-old first daughter really did seem enthusiastic and had displayed an impressive ability to work the crowd. She waded into her own section of the reception line, posing for photographs, shaking hands, signing autographs, leaning down to greet old ladies in wheelchairs and babies in strollers. She had the perfect posture, clasped hands and ever-present smile of someone who was accustomed to being stared at, and she seemed comfortable accepting the adulation of dozens of gawking strangers who jostled to meet her.

I'd put some of the Chelsea material into a spot story about Hillary starting the three-day visit to Long Island, and I'd hoped to get even better stuff for a feature. My brain was bouncing around phrases like "in her father's footsteps … like father, like daughter … the Clinton gene for pleasing the crowd," and I'd asked the photographer who was working with me to save whatever he didn't transmit yesterday to go with the story today.

The only problem was Chelsea. She simply wasn't cooperating with the story that I was writing in my mind. The day before she'd taken the initiative to work the crowd, approaching bystanders with her arm extended. But now, at the train station, while her mother positioned herself so she could catch commuters on their way to the platform, Chelsea had hung back, standing 15 feet away with a couple of aides, saying hi only when one of the people rushing by happened to notice her. She was perfectly polite and friendly when approached and even borrowed my pen to sign a couple of autographs. But it was clear that her heart wasn't in it. Then at the next stops, a restaurant and day camp, she'd made it clear that she was also off-limits to all of us. The real Chelsea had obliterated the Chelsea I'd profiled in my head, and my story was nowhere. And naturally, although we requested a Q-and-A with Chelsea, we didn't get one. While I could see why they didn't want to have Chelsea answering our questions, it also seemed unfair that they could trot her out as a big campaign prop but then deny us the right to get a few quotes.

I didn't know then that the day she'd spent working the line, chatting with everybody, would be one of the few days that she didn't seem like a robot. In October, she and her mother went to a senior citizens residence in Queens, and the lady who was emceeing the event sweetly asked Chelsea, who was doing her usual plastered-on smile and robotic-clap routine, if the audience could just hear the sound of her voice. The first daughter stepped up to the microphone and, sounding more like Ginger on "Gilligan's Island" than a senior at Stanford, uttered a breathy "Heh-low," then stepped away.

The audience was silent for a moment, expecting the oddly orphaned greeting to be followed by some conventional phrase like "It's so nice to be here" or "Thank you for your support for my mother." But that was it. Just "Heh-low" and nothing else. For the rest of the campaign, you could hear reporters covering Hillary muttering "Heh-low" to themselves at all hours of the day and night. On a long, boring string of meaningless events, even the grumpiest, hungriest, most exhausted journalist could manage a smile in response to that little "Heh-low."

Whether it was stage fright, indifference or something else that kept Chelsea from embracing her moment in the spotlight, I thought about Chelsea's odd "heh-low" years later when she was hired by NBC as a reporter. POLITICO reported that she was paid $600,000 a year by the network, even though she only did a couple of stories and didn't seem to have much chemistry with the camera. After three years on the job and mixed reviews, she left shortly before her daughter was born. It wasn't a stretch to imagine that she'd been hired partly because it would ensure the network access to her famous parents—but then the same could be said of Jenna Bush Hager, daughter of George W. Bush, who was also hired by NBC.

Back in the van with the Hillary crew, headed to our next stop, a news conference where Hillary was to be endorsed by Planned Parenthood (another moment from the 2000 campaign that seems unthinkable in the 21st century climate of controversy and violence surrounding Planned Parenthood), I whined to Bob Hardt of the Post: "What's the lead?"

"There is no lead," he responded matter-of-factly. "We're in a news-free zone."

Later I gave Frank Eltman, the AP reporter covering Lazio, the bad news that Karen Finney had made no progress helping me to complete the "favorites" story. This was of particular interest to Frank because he'd had no trouble getting Lazio's staff to help him finish his list a month earlier. The idea for the story was not particularly original, but it had grown out of a meeting we'd had with AP staff from upstate who'd told us that a lot of the local papers were becoming bored with the daily campaign stories. The story that got more play than just about anything else we'd done in recent times was Frank's account of Lazio falling in a Memorial Day parade and splitting his lip. At least it was a story about something real happening, instead of just another talking head. We brainstormed a little and somebody said it was too bad we couldn't ask Hillary the famous "boxers or briefs" question that a 17-year-old girl had asked Bill Clinton on MTV. The closest we could come to that, someone else had mused, was to ask her if she wore "cotton or nylon."

I knew I'd never have the nerve to ask Hillary what kind of underwear she wore. So in the end Frank and I came up with the list of uncontroversial favorites to ask the candidates. Frank got his answers right away: Lazio's staff took his tape recorder and had Lazio answer all the questions while the cassette was running, then gave the tape back to Frank. I thought I'd get through my list a short time later, when I and another AP staffer were granted a sit-down interview with Hillary in upstate Corning. After we got through the serious questions, I explained the "favorites" idea to her. She laughed and seemed amenable, so I started with the list, expecting a one- or two-word answer to everything. Instead I got a long story with everything.

Most people have a quick answer to "How do you take your coffee?" Not Hillary. Sometimes she takes her coffee black, she explained, other times with lots of cream, sometimes she likes espresso, sometimes cappuccino. You just couldn't pin Hillary down, not even on her coffee. Then there was the question about the worst job she'd ever had. Lazio had given a two-word answer: "Mosquito control."

But Hillary's worst-job story was a virtual parable of youthful righteousness. She'd been traveling with a friend around the country after college and had ended up in Alaska, where she got a job on a floating dock processing salmon. She was issued a raincoat, rubber boots and a spoon and was instructed to scoop the guts out of the fish. But she decided the fish didn't look all that healthy, and she sought out the manager to pass on her concerns.

Her complaints apparently spooked the owners, or maybe they really did have something to hide, because when she returned for her next shift, the whole fish-processing operation had disappeared without a trace. Strike one for Hillary the Moral Crusader! It was a good story, and oh-so-Hillary, but it took so long for her to tell it that by the time she was finished, Howard Wolfson told us the interview was over. That left me with seven or eight questions I hadn't had a chance to ask.

So Frank had his list done in an afternoon without even being in the candidate's presence. I'd had a coveted private sit-down with Hillary and hadn't gotten through half of it. I sent Howard an email asking for help in completing it. No response. A few days later, I sent him another email with the same non-result. When I found out about the Long Island trip, it seemed as if it might be the perfect opportunity to get someone on Hillary's staff to help me out the way Lazio's staff had assisted Frank. I felt kind of silly about it, of course; it seemed ridiculous to go to all this trouble to find out Hillary's favorite color. On the other hand, it was infuriating to me that it had become such a big deal when the questions were so short and straightforward and the Lazio list was long done.

I was thrilled when Karen Finney later agreed to help me. But when she told me a day later that she hadn't had a chance to pursue it, I started obsessing and even getting paranoid about it. Such a simple problem, yet I was so powerless to fix it. I began fantasizing that I would have to ask the questions one at a time at Hillary's press conferences. Everyone else would be asking about education policy or her stand on Israel, and I would be shouting out something about her favorite movie. Or maybe I would have to ask her on one of those rare occasions when she strolled over to say good morning before an event formally began. "Good morning, Mrs. Clinton," I imagined myself responding. "As long as you're standing here, do you mind if I ask you what your favorite junk food is?"

Interestingly, though, in the 2016 presidential campaign, her staff seemed to welcome these types of questions as a way to humanize her. She still fights the public perception that she's an ice queen, an iron lady and every other stereotype of the stiff, humorless, ball-busting female boss that has dogged her since first lady days.

Part of why it's persisted is that she's not naturally warm and fuzzy. Some candidates come across as authentic without even trying— like Florida's Republican Sen. Marco Rubio, who effortlessly sounds like a genuine Everyman when he talks about growing up with a dad who worked as a bartender and a mom who was a maid (even if he does get dinged by his opponents for his robotic anti-Obama lines). Hillary grew up in a normal, middle-class family, but her years as a member of the elite have given her a tin ear, like when she said in 2014 that she and Bill came out of the White House "dead broke"— never mind their speaking fees and million-dollar book contracts. So as she powered through a series of talk-show interviews in the 2015 run-up to the presidential race—dancing with Ellen DeGeneres, performing in a skit with Jimmy Fallon about Donald Trump and telling Stephen Colbert about binge-watching favorite shows like "The Good Wife" and "Madam Secretary," I naturally thought back to that elusive list of favorites and how hard it was to get her staff to help me get her answers.

Finally, though, it happened. One of her staff got the list completed and my story was done. Her favorite snack foods were chocolate and fruit, and her favorite color, she said, was yellow.

CHAPTER 10

Me and the First Lady
Talk Potty-Training

We didn't talk as much about work-life balance at the end of the 20th century as we do today, nor was there as much attention paid to the struggles of working moms—struggles that have led some women to give up careers in favor of staying home because it's so darn hard to juggle jobs and childrearing. Hillary did talk about some of these issues in the 2000 campaign, though, which I always found ironic, because I was spending a lot less time with my two young boys in order to cover the Senate race. Maybe it's fitting, then, that if I had to pinpoint one moment in the campaign that stands out for me personally, it would probably be this one: I not only talked to Hillary about potty-training my son, but the conversation was captured on videotape and it ended up on TV news. I'm certain that none of the men covering the Nixon-McGovern campaign in "The Boys on the Bus" ever came close to a conversation like that with the candidates of 1972.

• • •

The phone rang late one night in September 2000. It was my mother-in-law, Leah, who, despite her early run-in with Hillary's Secret Service agents and the phony-baloney Listening Tour, had remained very interested in the Senate campaign and my coverage.

"Beth? My friend just called to tell me that Hillary was on the Channel 2 news talking about how you potty-trained Nathaniel. How is that possible?"

"What?" I said. "What are you talking about?"

"My friend Bea told me she saw Hillary on Channel 2 news talking to the Associated Press reporter about potty-training, so she figured that had to be you, and she called me. Why was Hillary talking about that on TV?"

"Well, she asked me how my vacation was," I said, slowly trying to remember the rest of the conversation, "and I told her I'd potty-trained Nathaniel, but I didn't realize the cameras were rolling...."

My mother-in-law's friend Beatrice Hart had been right. The lead item on the WCBS-TV news had been a story about "The New Hillary," by their political correspondent, Marcia Kramer. The anchor's lead-in was, "She's shedding her old image and showing voters the kinder, gentler Hillary," and the entire piece was about how she'd invited us all to go have coffee with her one morning after she'd held a press conference with Robert F. Kennedy Jr. to get his personal endorsement. The event was held in Manhattan's Riverside Park, on a narrow path with the Hudson River on one side. It was a relatively remote spot, with few passersby, making it an ideal location for a Casual Hillary Moment. She couldn't be mobbed here, and the Secret Service agents appeared to be as relaxed as they ever were, displaying none of their usual obsessions with controlling where we were standing or moving.

That day just happened to be my first day back on the beat after a vacation in Maine, where my sister and I have a summer cottage in a rural area. Most of the reporters covering the Senate campaign had skipped their summer vacations and were instead planning exotic vacations for after November in the Caribbean, Morocco and Spain, but my older son Danny would be in the middle of the school year by the time this was over, and it didn't seem fair to deprive him and his brother of our annual summer trip to the country just because I was covering Hillary. Besides, the opinions of our friends and relatives in Maine often provide a dose of reality from our big-city mindset. I asked one of my aunts, who lives in a small town in Maine and worked in a shoe factory for many years while raising seven children, what she thought of the presidential candidates, and she replied, "Well, I don't know who Gore thinks is going to vote for him if he raises the tax on cigarettes." Now there's a point of view you'd never hear on the Upper West Side of Manhattan.

I was glad to see the other reporters that day in Riverside Park; I'd come to think of most of them as friends. A couple of them asked me what I'd done when I was away, and to the two mothers of young children in the group, Liz Moore of Newsday and Andrea Bernstein of WNYC-AM radio, the National Public Radio affiliate, I explained that I had taken advantage of my rare sojourn as a full-time mommy to toilet train my 2-year-old. Liz had just done the same with her youngest, and Andrea proudly announced that her 2-year-old was using the potty, too.

A few minutes later, after the press conference with RFK Jr., Hillary motioned to us to follow her a few steps away to a cafe in the park. "C'mon," she said, "let's go have coffee!" She was in a relaxed, expansive mood; she'd made small talk with Marcia about taking a lot of vitamins to get through the final weeks of the campaign, tried on Andrea's headphones, and waved to a couple of people gliding by in a boat on the sparkling blue water. She sat down with the cafe proprietor, who earlier that morning had walked over to where she was holding the news conference and introduced himself as someone who strongly supported her campaign. All of a sudden as Hillary looked around at us, her eyes fixed on me. I guess after covering her for nearly two years, she'd noticed my absence over the past few weeks and took note of my return. "Hi, Beth!" she called out cheerily. "How was your vacation?"

Since I'd just finished telling the potty-training story to the other moms in the press corps, it was still on the tip of my tongue. "It was great!" I responded without hesitation. "I potty-trained my 2-year-old!"

"You did what?" she said.

All of a sudden it hit me that I should probably have given a more conventional answer like, "It was so relaxing!" But now it was too late.

"I potty-trained my 2-year-old," I replied in a small voice.

Hillary looked at me expectantly, as if she still wasn't sure she'd heard me right. Then she repeated it back to me. "You potty-trained your 2-year-old?"

I swallowed and nodded. A second earlier, chatting with the other moms in the press corps, it had seemed as if talking about potty-training was the most natural thing in the world. But now that Hillary had repeated it back to me, I was starting to feel ridiculous. I mean, I had just told the first lady that I potty-trained my 2-year-old! What an absurd thing to do! What the hell was wrong with me?

But I needn't have worried. Now that Hillary realized she'd heard me right, she looked around at the small group and said emphatically, with a big smile, "This woman deserves a round of applause!" Then she turned back to me. "Boy or girl, Beth?"

"Boy," I answered, not sure whether it was better to disappear from the face of the earth at that point or soldier on.

"Boy? That's even harder!" she replied, laughing, then turned her attention elsewhere.

Marcia Kramer included the exchange in her Channel 2 segment on "The New Hillary" to show that Hillary was trying to make connections with us, to humanize herself, and that when she dropped the formality and the regal air, she could be warm and funny and caring, and, yes, even at ease in a conversation about potty-training. I still felt slightly foolish, but I also couldn't help but wonder: If it had been Chuck Schumer or Al D'Amato or Mayor Giuliani that I was covering instead of Hillary, and one of them had asked me how my vacation had been, would it have seemed as natural to mention potty-training? And if I had, would they actually have bothered to continue the discussion as if it were a perfectly legitimate topic, the way Hillary did, or would they have put me in a slot in their minds for keeping track of mentally unbalanced reporters and moved on to someone else?

I later talked to Marcia about why she had chosen to focus on how Hillary had reached out to us, instead of leading, as I had in the story I wrote that day for the AP, with RFK Jr.'s endorsement. Marcia said Hillary's informality with us that day "came at a time when people were beginning to wonder about that, and it gave her a humanity that maybe she hadn't had in the minds of voters. Seeing her stop a kid in the park and talk about sneakers and sitting down for coffee with the enemy (the reporters covering her), where she was buying, and passing the cream and asking if you needed sugar and playing hostess in a restaurant, was at some level bizarre in the context of the campaign. But she was also being totally personal. And she used little tidbits of our lives to appear to be more personal ... I totally understand why you were talking about the potty-training of your child. Could a male candidate have done that? If it was Chuck Schumer, he probably would have found some other level of common ground—not hearth and home and family. Maybe something about Brooklyn or 'Hey, I was out in Prospect Park the other day playing Frisbee with my kids' as opposed to this. It wouldn't have been a woman-to-woman issue. It would have been a safer issue."

And in a way, it seemed only right that Hillary should hear about my kids, since they ended up hearing so much about her. One day when I went to pick up Nathaniel from day care, the director informed me that my little son had that morning announced, "My mommy went to work. And Hillary's running for Senate!"

A few weeks later my older son was sick at school and the teacher asked him whom she should call to come get him, his mommy or his daddy.

"Better call my daddy, he's a lawyer," Danny replied.

"Why? What does your mom do?" the teacher said.

"She's covering Hillary."

"Hillary who?"

"You know. Hillary! The president's wife!"

"But what do you mean, she's covering Hillary?"

He shrugged. "I don't know. That's just what she does. She's covering Hillary."

Around the same time, Danny's Hebrew school teacher had asked the kids to make Rosh Hashanah cards for their parents for the Jewish New Year. I was amused but also slightly horrified to see the message Danny wrote inside: "Dear mom I hope you have a Happy time covering Hillary OK? Danny."

Both of my kids also pointed out Hil's picture in the newspaper without any prompting from me, and the little one had become so accustomed to my bringing campaign ads home with me on videotape to watch at night that sometimes when I went to put a regular tape in the VCR, he'd say, "Is that gonna be Hillary?"

There were also many evenings when I wrote my stories on the subway after leaving the office and then dictated them by cellphone while pushing Nathaniel's stroller on the way to get Danny from his after-school center. One evening I pored over campaign finance filings while sitting on the bench in a playground where the boys were soaking up the last bit of daylight before sundown. And many times I bribed them with candy and quarters to please, please be quiet while I just took one important phone call at home.

Not only did my children know all about Hillary, but when I flew up to Corning to take part in the AP's big sit-down interview with her, I found out that Hillary knew about my children. I was in a hotel conference room with a photographer and the AP reporter who usually covered her upstate when she walked in. I was surprised to hear her ask me about my kids right after we said hello. "They know all about you," I said, smiling.

"Well, I bet they do, because I'm always taking you away from them," she replied sweetly. Then she asked me their names, said she had "something for them," pulled out a book and a pen and began writing on the flyleaf.

"Dear Danny and Nathaniel," she wrote in a flowing cursive. "Best wishes, Hillary Clinton." Then she handed it to me. It was a copy of "Dear Socks, Dear Buddy."

I was completely taken aback. Journalists are not supposed to accept gifts from the people they cover. If you go out to eat with someone you're writing about, you're supposed to pick up the tab. If a public relations firm sends you some type of merchandise, you either give it away, return it or throw it out.

I briefly considered handing the book back to Hillary with an explanation of how I wasn't permitted to accept gifts, but that just seemed rude, especially since she'd already written my kids' names in it. Besides, our time with Hillary was strictly limited. We had a half-hour or so for our interview; I couldn't really justify taking up another five minutes with an argument over whether it was OK for me to take the book.

In one way, the book was a nice gesture on her part. Hillary often talked about the challenges of making society and the workplace more accommodating to working parents, and this was a direct acknowledgment on her part of the juggling I was doing. But I also felt angry that she'd put me in this awkward position.

Didn't Hillary or her staff know better than to go around giving presents to journalists? I started worrying that I'd be in trouble at work for not having self-righteously handed it back to her while announcing, "You can't buy me off with a present, Mrs. Clinton." Of course, then I'd be putting her in an uncomfortable position, and she or her staff might take it out on me by giving us even less access than we already had. It was just all too complicated, and I wished that she'd never given me anything. In the end I just thanked her in a small voice, put the book in my bag, and we turned on our tape recorders and went ahead with the interview.

The book felt as if it weighed about 50 pounds as I carried it home through the airports. I couldn't wait to tell my editors and let them decide whether I needed to return it. But their reactions were so nonchalant that I felt ridiculous all over again. "That book has about a $2 value," the news editor said to me dismissively when I guiltily presented the book for a verdict. "She probably gets cartons of them to give away." My bureau chief, Sam Boyle, agreed, explaining that a book given by the author fell under the category of a "token" and therefore didn't need to be returned.

I hadn't yet shown the book to my kids, but now that I'd gotten clearance, I could let them see it without feeling guilty. "Look," I told them, "Hillary sent you a present. It's a book about the pets who live in the White House with her and the president."

My older son wasn't much interested, but the little one looked at the pictures and then at me. "Hillary have a puppy and a pussycat?" he asked hopefully. I nodded.

A month later Hillary spoke at Metropolitan AME Church in Harlem, an all-black congregation. She always seemed at home in places of worship (although she pronounced the word like a Midwesterner, so that it sounded as if she were saying "warship," which drove me crazy); she knew her Bible and could easily quote chapter and verse, expounding on the reading of the day with unpretentious ease.

On this particular Sunday at Metropolitan, the reading for the day was about Joshua being chosen to lead the Jews after Moses died. The pastor, Robert Bailey, got up again and told his flock that God had given them a second chance to elect another Clinton. Hillary, he said, was their Joshua.

"Did you hear this lady?" he intoned. "We need Hillary Clinton in the White House!"

Behind him, U.S. Rep. Charlie Rangel, the longtime Harlem Democrat, started calling out "The Senate!" every time Bailey said "the White House." But the pastor couldn't hear him and just kept repeating "the White House."

Hillary, seated behind the pastor, facing the congregation (and the press), appeared totally stone-faced. Her eyes were downcast and unblinking and she sat completely still. For months her enemies had been saying that what she really wanted was not to serve in the Senate but to run for president, and that she would use the Senate as a steppingstone to try for the White House later. If there had been a spy in the audience videotaping the event for the Republicans, it would have made a perfect Hillary hate-ad: her sitting silently in a church while a black pastor says over and over again, "We need Hillary Clinton in the White House!" and the congregation cheering in response.

Her torture ended after a few moments when a deacon ran up to the lectern and whispered something in the pastor's ear. Bailey paused for a minute, then called out, "We want her in the Senate!" A relieved smile came over her face.

That night at home I was telling my husband the story over dinner and had just gotten to the part where the preacher keeps repeating "the White House," when my 2-year-old stood up on his chair. "You know what, Daddy?" he started saying. "You know what?"

"Just a minute," I said. "Let me finish telling this story—"

"You know what?" Now he was jumping up and down in his chair. "Hillary have a puppy dog and a pussycat! You know that, Daddy?"

At that moment I realized my life had truly been taken over by Hillary. Not only was I telling my husband Hillary stories over dinner, but my 2-year-old was interrupting me to tell his own Hillary stories.

Only much later did I find out that Hillary had given small gifts to many of my other colleagues, too. After Hillary had visited all 62 counties, she presented Gregg Birnbaum and Eileen Murphy with "Longevity Awards" for making it to more of the counties than any of the other reporters. At the same time, during this little presentation to the press corps in the lobby of a Holiday Inn in Plattsburgh, the rest of the reporters on the trail that day got caps that said "Hillary Clinton." Of course, no reporter would be caught dead wearing a hat or a pin or a T-shirt with a candidate's name on it.

Gregg later determined that the caps were made in the Dominican Republic and tried to figure out which factory they had come from in case it turned out to be a sweatshop or an operation using child labor. But he was never able to pin it down.

My older son, Danny, meanwhile, had been lobbying for a long time to accompany me on assignment to a Hillary event. I felt a little funny about doing it for several reasons. One, I had a serious job to do at these events, and I couldn't take the chance that he might somehow disrupt the proceedings or take my attention away from what she was saying or doing. Two, I thought he might get very bored very fast, and most of these events were part of a long day of campaigning. There was no easy way to bring him to one small program and then somehow get him back home without taking me away from my need to either go back to the office and write the story up, or go on to the next event.

And three, it seemed a slightly gray area for me to use my privilege as a journalist to bring a relative into a campaign event that would otherwise not be open to the public. After all, I didn't take Danny's grandma into that Listening Tour event—how could I now justify bringing him to a press conference or a fundraiser?

On the other hand, if I was going to disrupt their young lives as much as I had by devoting myself to covering this campaign, in some ways it seemed only fair to let them experience the cause of the disruption firsthand. Even what I made for dinner each night depended on Hillary. My meal plan for the week included some dinners that required prep time for cutting up vegetables or lighting the oven, some that involved nothing more than throwing a package of frozen pasta in a pot of boiling water, and one night set aside for getting takeout food delivered to my door. If I had an early day with Hillary and actually got home by 6 p.m., I'd plan on a prep-time dinner. If I had a late day, it was a frozen-pasta night. The takeout was my emergency crutch, to be saved for the nights when I was not only late coming home, but everything else went wrong, too: the train got stuck in the tunnel, Nathaniel was crying, Danny had a ton of homework, the kids needed baths, the garbage and the laundry baskets were both overflowing and the VCR wasn't working.

"Is the deliveryman coming tonight?" Nathaniel would ask hopefully if we were caught in the rain without an umbrella or the phone started ringing the minute we walked in the door. On those nights, instead of rushing through the door to get dinner going, I'd just collapse on the sofa, wallet in hand and wait for the doorbell to herald the arrival of chicken sate from our local Thai restaurant.

Sure, Hillary had been a working mother, resuming her law practice in Arkansas after just a few months of maternity leave for Chelsea, and I'd heard her tell stories about being stuck in a late-afternoon meeting the day of an important school play, but I wondered if she'd ever had to pull a juggling act like this in the governor's mansion.

One day in the fall when the quarterly Federal Election Commission reports were due, both campaigns had scheduled to release their campaign finance documents late in the afternoon. I should have known it wasn't going to happen that way, that it would be delayed, and I'd have to get my husband to pick the kids up. But for some reason I stupidly thought I'd actually be on the subway in time to get the boys.

By the time I found out that the Clinton reports were delayed by a Xerox machine breaking down at Kinko's and that the staffer who'd been sent to fetch the Lazio documents was taking longer than expected to return, I couldn't reach my husband. I phoned a neighbor to pick Danny up, then began a frantic back-and-forth with the long-suffering director of Nathaniel's day care center. Eventually I got on the subway carrying a huge carton of documents, and at the point where the D train from Manhattan to Brooklyn emerged from the tunnel onto the bridge, I pulled out my cellphone and called the day care center for the umpteenth time to see if my husband had come to the rescue yet. He hadn't. It was already by then 6:45 p.m., not all that late in the life of a normal person, but I felt terrible that the day care director was sitting there 45 minutes after she was supposed to have left just because I couldn't get there in time to pick my child up.

By the time we all got home around 7:30 p.m., I had to lock myself in a bedroom and start combing through the documents, then pull out my laptop and try to write a coherent story while Danny banged on the door to ask if I could come help him with just one little thing in his homework.

If I'd had any illusions that I was leading a glamorous existence covering a celebrity, they crashed right then and there. I wasn't chasing deadlines; I was chasing third-grade homework, bubble baths and dinner that could be made in 15 minutes or less while a screaming toddler grabbed onto my leg.

I have to pause here and give a small thank-you to several members of the Clinton campaign who did what they could to support my juggling efforts. One day when I was desperately trying to leave the office, I got word that the Clinton campaign was about to release a new ad.

This necessitated my picking up a videotape at their headquarters and my writing an analysis of the ad. I emailed Howard asking when the ad would be ready.

"Please keep it under your hat for a bit," he wrote back.

"I'm not pressing for it," I responded. "On the other hand, I'm probably walking out the door at 4:30, so if I need to plan a stop at your office on my way home, I need to know. Sorry, but it's the old conflicting-values dilemma. Hillary on the one hand. Seven-year-old Danny and 2-year-old Nathaniel on the other… "

Two minutes later, another message from Howard. "Release is going out now. Ads should be available at the office presently. I vote for the kids, by the way."

On a few other occasions when Hillary had an event that wasn't important enough for me to staff myself and was so late or in such a remote location that it wasn't even worth getting someone else from my office to fill in for me, Hillary's staff was nice enough to call me at home, by cellphone, just before she began speaking so that I could monitor her speech from home. I only did it two or three times, early on in the campaign, but each time it was a lifesaver, enabling me to keep tabs on the candidate while spending the evening with my kids.

Of course, I wasn't required to cover the campaign. I could have declined the assignment and stuck to the kinds of stories where I'd be able to leave work every day promptly after putting in my eight hours. But I'm hoping that my children, in the long run, benefit from having a mother who had an interesting career. Nobody ever wonders whether fathers with demanding jobs are doing their children a disservice.

One day, Dean Murphy of The New York Times brought his 6-year-old son, Christian, to spend a day on the campaign trail going with us to black churches, riding around in the van and even attending a press conference. "Christian never asked to meet Mrs. Clinton, he just wanted to see what Daddy did every day," Dean later told me.

Still, he shared my concerns about whether it was appropriate to let your kid tag along with somebody famous just because you're assigned to cover the person. Dean even sought (and received) his editor's approval to do it. A couple of the photographers in the press corps snapped a picture of little Christian shaking Hillary's hand when she noticed him standing in front of the pack at the news conference, but Dean decided not to ask her to autograph the picture. "I just didn't feel right making that request while covering the race," he said. "My wife has her copy of 'It Takes a Village' and would have liked an autograph as well, but I didn't bring that along either."

Christian was better-behaved than some of the journalists that day; he never showed any restlessness during those long church sermons. He also displayed an impressive instinctual understanding of the photo-op concept, turning his face directly to the cameras as his picture was taken. But I think the funniest part of Christian's day with us was that, when it was over, he asked Dean, "Daddy, why does she say the same thing every place she goes?"

Eventually, the appropriate venue presented itself for me to bring Danny along. My husband is on the board of directors of a housing organization called Good Old Lower East Side. Before becoming a lawyer, he'd worked there as a tenant organizer, and he'd remained involved in the years since he'd left. In late October, he got a telephone message from GOLES inviting him to attend a forum Hillary was holding in a church on the Lower East Side for tenant leaders and housing activists. It was scheduled to take place mid-evening, a few hours after her third and final televised debate with Lazio. I had to cover the debate and also planned to attend the housing forum even though I was fairly certain it would generate no news. Our coverage that day would by necessity have to focus on the debate.

So this seemed, at last, like the perfect opportunity for Danny and Nathaniel to see the woman who had been dominating their home lives for so many months. Their father would be there to deal with the kids if they misbehaved; I wasn't likely to be writing a story about the event anyway; and because their dad's invitation had nothing to do with me, they had a legitimate reason to attend.

We met up outside the church, and when we got in, I realized that most of the press was seated upstairs. "Oh, Mommy, I wanna go up there with you!" Danny whined. "Please!"

Their father stayed downstairs with the invitees and Nathaniel, while Danny and I headed up to the balcony. A Secret Service agent was posted on the steps to search everyone's bag. The photographer ahead of me was firing test flashes in her camera for him and unscrewing her lenses, and I took out my tape recorder and cellphone and turned them on to prove that they were regular electronic devices and not explosives. It had all become routine by now, but of course Danny watched intently with his eyes wide open. "Why do you have to do this, Mommy? What's going on?"

I explained that Hillary is a very important person and this gentleman who was looking in everyone's bags was supposed to protect her and make sure nobody was bringing in anything dangerous. Danny nodded and then started shoving his hands into each of his pockets. A moment later he produced a blue rubber ball from the cargo pocket of his jeans and with a smile proudly held it out to the agent to be inspected.

I introduced him to some of the other reporters, and Edward Lewine of the Daily News was nice enough to let him play with his tape recorder.

They interviewed each other and then we played Hangman on my notepad. Every now and then, I'd hear Nathaniel cry out, "Mommy!" and look up to try to find me in the balcony. It was going to be a long night.

Finally Hillary arrived. I saw her eyes rove up to the balcony to where we were all seated; she often took a quick glance at the press corps before starting. I couldn't be sure, but it looked to me as if she were looking at Danny, trying to figure out who he was. I put my arm around him and pointed to his head and then to me. She smiled and Danny waved at her.

She began speaking and within two minutes Danny was bored. "When is it going to be over?" he whispered.

I groaned. I should have known this was going to happen. "Danny, be quiet, you just have to sit through it. I really have to pay attention now. It'll be over in a little while."

He started moving around the balcony and accidentally poked my elbow. I'd had my notepad and a bunch of papers resting on the ledge of the balcony, and his hitting my arm caused me to push the whole thing over the ledge. I watched in horror as the notebook landed with a thud amid the seats below us and the papers fluttered down, one by one. A couple of the other reporters started laughing. I leaned over the balcony at the people who were seated below as they looked up to see what the hell was going on. The commotion put the Secret Service agent on high alert, too; I saw him looking at me intently, trying to figure out if he should take me out then and there or give me a second chance. "I'm sorry! I'm sorry! It was an accident! I'm so sorry!" I kept whispering as loudly as I could as the people downstairs glared up at me.

There was no point in getting mad at Danny. I should have known something like this would happen. I ordered him to sit far away from the edge of the balcony and moved myself back, too. I had an extra notebook in my bag and took it out, but there was no need. A minute later, someone from the audience appeared next to me holding the papers I'd dropped over the edge. I thanked her profusely, and she looked at Danny and smiled. They'd figured out what had happened and were being nice about it.

Then it was over. Hillary stayed around to shake hands, and Danny and I headed downstairs. The boys wanted to meet her. Again, I felt the conflict. Was this OK, or was it over the line? "The line" was such a vague, tricky thing. You didn't want to be in a position of seeking or receiving personal favors. But when you'd spent as much time covering someone as I had Hillary, and the person becomes, in some way, a part of your life, the way my children had become intrigued with her, some amount of personal interaction seemed only natural. I found my husband, put Nathaniel on my shoulders, took Danny's hand, and waded into the mob of people waiting to shake Hillary's hand. "Hillary! Hillary!" I could hear the little one calling her name when she neared us. She looked up and waved at him, then reached over and shook Danny's hand. One of her press aides, Cathie Levine, spotted us and motioned us through the line to a vestibule where I introduced them a few minutes later and guiltily snapped a quick picture. A few days later, I read in USA Today that the reporters covering George W. Bush frequently asked him to autograph a card, photo or poster, and that he willingly posed for photos with reporters' relatives at various stops around the country. That made me feel better. If it was OK in the presidential corps, then it was probably OK to do what I had done.

But there was a funny ending to that evening in the church with my kids. My son Nathaniel, who had famously just completed potty-training a month or so earlier, told his dad he had to pee. So they went to the bathroom after the boys were done saying hi to Hillary, only to find a Secret Service agent posted outside the bathroom door. "Sorry," the guy said. "You'll have to wait 15 minutes." Apparently the bathroom was in lockdown mode in case Her Majesty needed to use it.

"But my son needs to pee! He can't wait 15 minutes!" my husband said.

The guy shrugged. "Sorry."

This section of the Lower East Side was relatively deserted in those days. It's not as if there were a restaurant next store, or even in the next block, that we could have run into to use. So we did what any parents would do in the interest of avoiding wet pants: We took Nathaniel outside and let him pee in a vacant lot.

But in a lot of venues like fancy hotels or small upstate restaurants, the Secret Service did not put the bathroom in lockdown, and a number of stories actually involved press corps encounters with Hillary in the ladies' room. Anna Quindlen once wrote a column for The New York Times in which she noted that as a female reporter in the largely male press corps covering City Hall, she'd had "years of worrying that the best stories were coming out of conversations in the men's room" between the mayor, his male staff and the male reporters. But other than an encounter by Gail Sheehy, who began one of the chapters of "Hillary's Choice" with the words "I ran into her in the ladies' room," I don't think any of the interactions anybody on the campaign ever had with Hillary in a bathroom ever made it into our coverage. Yet these run-ins were noteworthy, if only because there was something forbidden about them. We couldn't ride on her van or take her picture on her plane, we couldn't get her on the phone like a normal candidate, but, hey, if she had to pee and one of us had to pee at the same time, you could very well find yourself in the privacy of a bathroom with the very private first lady.

Lara Jakes of the Albany Times Union, who turned 26 shortly after she was assigned to cover Hillary's campaign, actually followed the first lady into a restroom on the very first leg of the Listening Tour.

"I kind of got goaded into doing it," she recalled. "The guys on the bus were like, 'Jakes, go in there! Ya gotta see what's going on in there.'"

So Lara followed Hillary in at a rest stop on Route 88 between Binghamton and Pindars Corners. Hillary's personal assistant Kelly Craighead, a funny, lively woman with long blond hair who could also be as tough and protective of Hillary as any of the Secret Service agents, was standing by the sink as the first lady emerged from a stall.

"They're both giving me the hairy eyeball, looking at my tape recorder," Lara recalled. "I said something like, 'I'm not gonna ambush you in the bathroom. I'm just gonna make sure no news happens.' While she's washing her hands, this middle-aged woman with two daughters comes rushing into the back stall. Hillary and Kelly leave. The woman finishes helping her daughters and I say, 'Did you realize that was Hillary Clinton in there?' The woman goes, 'Oh my God, that was the first lady.' One of her daughter's names happens to be Hillary, and they go running out to find her."

Meanwhile when Lara got back on the press bus, she wasn't sure if she'd let down her colleagues or not. "I mean, this was my first real big political race," she said. "They send me in here to the bathroom and I don't know if I'm supposed to ask her about Whitewater or what. I'm thinking, 'What if I blow this?' We've got a year and a half to go in this race, and I just don't really feel comfortable asking her questions in the ladies' room. I kept thinking, 'What would a guy do?'"

Liz Moore also had a ladies' room encounter one day when we were at the Waldorf. She walked into the bathroom, saw Kelly at the sink, and realized that Hillary was in a stall. "I couldn't deal with it," she confessed when she came back to the press area. "I turned around and walked out."

"You did the nice thing," I told her. "You were just being human."

Eileen Murphy, who can do a wickedly funny imitation of Hillary saying just about anything, had a bathroom story, too. She was in a ladies' room somewhere upstate one day, mocking one of Hillary's anti-Giuliani phrases like, "Reject the politics of derision and divisiveness!"—and at the same time trying on a pair of Gucci sunglasses she'd just found.

Kelly Craighead and Karen Finney were in the bathroom with her, telling her the sunglasses looked good. "I'm practicing the politics of destruction on myself!" she said, then noticed that the door to one of the stalls was opening.

All of a sudden, Hillary emerged, smiling.

CHAPTER 11

Harriet Tubman, Hillary and the Black Vote

It's hard to imagine, in light of Hillary Clinton's loss to Barack Obama in the 2008 campaign, how beloved she was by black voters when she ran for Senate. Gloria Steinem, in her recent memoir, blamed the media for reducing the 2008 campaign for the Democratic presidential nomination to one of gender vs. race, "polarizing the constituencies of two barrier-breaking firsts." A 2015 "Saturday Night Live" parody put it more bluntly, with the actress playing Hillary saying, "In 2008 of course I lost, but I was running against a cool black guy." In 2016, the spoof continued, Hillary hoped to be "the cool black guy"—meaning that her quest to become the first female president might give her the edge over her male rivals.

The racial dynamic was different in the 2000 Senate race. Back then, Hillary not only had her husband's cred as a friend of the black community, but she was appealing to black New Yorkers at a time when race relations in New York City were perceived to be worsening partly because of the policies and pronouncements of Mayor Rudolph Giuliani. Hillary benefited from this perception even after Giuliani dropped out of the Senate race. And because the turnout of black voters can make or break a candidate in New York, her campaign made it a priority to remind the black community that Hillary needed them to come out in big numbers on Election Day if she was going to be assured a win.

Here's a look at how she connected with that constituency on her tour of black churches, and how the media reacted.

Every Sunday between Labor Day and Election Day in 2000, Hillary went to black churches. Some days we started with the 7 a.m. service and hit our sixth or seventh church around mid-afternoon, but on this day, the schedule was light: just three churches before noon.

We began at Memorial Baptist Church in Harlem. It wasn't one of the powerhouse churches Democratic politicians usually visit, but then, Hillary wasn't content to hit a half-dozen churches like a normal candidate. Instead, in the two months leading up to Nov. 7, she hit 27 black churches, from storefront tabernacles with peeling paint in neighborhoods where few white politicians ventured, to better-known places like Abyssinian Baptist in Harlem, run by the Rev. Calvin Butts, a prominent activist and power broker who once made headlines by calling Giuliani a "racist."

The row of seats taken up by the press corps was just about the only part of the church occupied by white faces. Occasionally a black photographer or reporter was part of the mix, but on that particular day, we were not only mostly white, we were also largely Jewish. And because it was the Sunday after Rosh Hashanah, we greeted each other by saying "Happy New Year!"

Most of the worshipers were on their feet, clapping, singing and rocking to an electric guitar, piano and drum ensemble driven by the steady, happy jangle of a tambourine. "Lift Him up!" the several hundred voices sang as one, and within minutes, I and most of the other reporters stood up, too, clapping and swaying along with them; the music was irresistible. Still, we were interlopers, journalists in a place of worship and mostly white people in a place filled with black faces, and no matter what we did, we felt self-conscious.

Soon the booming sounds died away and we sat down. The Rev. Preston Washington got up and shouted, "Let's give them all the news!" and the congregation let out a cheer in response.

The reporter sitting next to me gave me a look of mock bewilderment.

"Did he just say, 'Let's welcome all the Jews'?"

I stifled a laugh. "No, he said, 'Let's give them all the news.' All the news, as in the Gospel, not all the Jews."

Now Hillary appeared at the podium, a small, familiar blond figure in her going-to-church navy blue suit with the skirt hem falling just below her knees. It was the Sunday version of her black pantsuit. A tumultuous cheer went up, and a warm, wide, toothy, lipsticked smile bloomed across her face.

"She's gonna win," declared the pastor. "And we are going to come out in droves for her."

It was a point that needed to be made. Nobody doubted that black voters preferred Hillary over Lazio. But a strong black turnout was essential if her win was to be guaranteed.

"Whoooo!" Hillary hooted as the applause died down and she looked around, feeling the love. "Thank you for the day the Lord has made!"

It was her standard opening line, a riff on the psalm that begins, "This is the day the Lord has made; let us rejoice and be glad in it."

"My Baptist husband says 'Good morning!'" she continued. (Hillary, as anyone in the press corps and most of the people in this church could tell you, is Methodist.) The reference to Bill, whose popularity in the black community was legendary, unleashed another ovation.

She threw out a few thank-yous to local politicians in the audience, most of them introduced as "my good friend" so-and-so, then lowered her voice and eyes, taking on a solemn aspect that was immediately sensed by the congregation, which became completely silent and respectful and still.

"I want to thank you," she said in a small, humble, grateful voice, "for the prayers and support and good wishes you have given me and my husband and my daughter over the last eight years. Those prayers have uplifted, sustained, and, I believe, protected us."

A smattering of applause and a murmur of acknowledgment rippled through the congregation. The first lady of the United States, the most famous woman in the world, had not only found her way to their small church on 115th Street this morning, but now she was thanking them.

Of course, the first few times I heard Hillary thank her black supporters for their prayers, I wasn't entirely sure what she was referring to. Then one day, when I was standing outside a restaurant where she was holding a private meeting, a black lady who was part of the crowd outside waiting to greet her came up to me and, unprompted, explained it.

"Everybody loves her husband," she told me. "There were so many churches that fasted and prayed for him during the impeachment. Because they believed he was a good president. He's human. But he's for the people. And I think she's a very good wife to stick with him. People say she did it for the power. But she did it because marriage is for better or for worse."

I thanked the woman and made a mental note to spend more time talking to ladies on street corners in Queens and less time talking to political analysts on the phone in Washington.

Back to Hillary's speech at Memorial Baptist: Now she was reciting statistics from the Clinton administration's economic miracle—the lowest child-poverty level on record. The lowest level of black unemployment on record. More applause, then the self-congratulations gave way to a humble message in keeping with the spirit of a religious service.

"But I don't believe that America is called upon to be the richest nation," she said, pausing as a few voices called back, "That's right!" and "You tell it!"

"I believe it is called upon to be the best," she continued. "And I believe our best days are ahead of us. That's why I'm running for the Senate. I want to be part of making that future."

Now we were about to hear the press corps' favorite part of Hillary's Standard Sunday Morning Sermon. She started by noting that she'd been to all 62 counties in New York state, and that one of the many places she visited along the way was Auburn, to see the house that Harriet Tubman had lived in after escaping slavery.

Harriet Tubman, Hillary added, "is one of my favorite heroines in American history. Because when she got to freedom, she didn't say, 'Well, I'm free. I'm just gonna sit back and live the good life,' did she?"

"No, she didn't," several voices responded.

"She decided to go back to the South and bring more escaped slaves to freedom," Hillary continued.

"Mm-hmmm!" the worshipers called back.

Now Hillary's voice dropped to a stage whisper and she looked conspiratorially around the room, as if we were all on the Underground Railroad with Hillary and Harriet. Everyone became still again.

"She'd tell people to meet her at night in a swamp or a grove of willow trees. And she'd say, 'If you hear the dogs, keep going!'" Hillary said, her voice slowly rising.

"Yes! Yes!" the audience called back.

I didn't need to take notes anymore. I just wrote "Keep going!" in my notebook, put my pen down and listened for the words that I and every other reporter here knew by heart.

"If you hear the gunfire, keep going! If you hear the men shouting, keep going! If you hear the footsteps, keep going!" She got louder and louder to be heard over the growing din, but her cadence was as perfect as a real preacher's, every pause timed just right to allow for a response from the audience. We white reporters sitting in the back row may have felt we didn't belong here, but that white lady in the front of the church, she was perfectly at home. She knew how to reach this audience, and they sensed that she respected them. It didn't hurt her comfort level that she'd spent years going around to churches in Arkansas with Bill. And it didn't hurt that she'd been on the campaign trail for more than a year. In the early days of covering Hillary, we talked a lot about her tin ear. She'd drone on too long, she'd say the wrong thing, her message was clunky or vague. But in politics as in school, there is a learning curve, and we were seeing the result of it then. By that point, the first lady had perfect pitch, and her routine was going over big time with the fans.

"We all have to keep going until we are a just nation," she said, practically shouting now as people began to stand, cheering and clapping and loving every word out of her mouth. "But I need your help. And if you will help me, I will be there for you!"

Now she quieted down again in preparation for the grand finale.

"Because there is one thing you know about me," she said softly, then roared: "When I tell you I'll stick with you, I'll stick with you!"

As it always did, this line brought the house down. The first time I heard her say it, in a church in Brooklyn, I almost didn't believe what I was hearing. What exactly did that mean, "When I tell you I'll stick with you, I'll stick with you"? It appeared to be a veiled reference to her marriage. But that seemed absurd. Why would a woman who had gone out of her way to avoid explaining why she stayed with Bill suddenly be boasting about it? I asked a couple of the other reporters sitting near me that day for their interpretation and found them about evenly divided between those who thought it was about her marriage and those who thought it wasn't. So I went outside and started asking people as they left church. What was she talking about when she said, "When I tell you I'll stick with you, I'll stick with you"?

"The average person took that to mean, 'I stood behind my husband,'" said one man.

"She had a right to stick with him," a lady told me. "And that means no matter how hard the situation is, she will hang in there for us."

I thought back to that day two years ago, the first day I ever covered Hillary, when everyone in America was gossiping about Monica and Bill, and she held court at a conference on global economics and pretended that the world outside didn't exist. Now I was covering her running for office, and she was using her marriage as a metaphor for political loyalty. She'd figured out how to take that doormat thing and turn it into a virtue. She was either shameless, or a genius, or both.

Back at Memorial, the church exploded with applause as she delivered her final exhortation: "Let's keep going! Let's have a great big turnout in the election! If you fight for me in the next five weeks,

I will go to the Senate and fight for you for the next six years! Thank you, everybody! Thank you so-o-o-o-o much!"

The band started up again and the applause turned into rhythmic clapping in time to the beat. The first lady and her entourage swept out of the church, with us Jews and the rest of the press corps scrambling to follow and pile into the van before it pulled away from the curb behind the Hillary Speedwagon, en route to the next church. The very back seat in these vans is always the last to fill up, not only because it's hard to get to, climbing over everybody's legs and shoulders and knapsacks and cameras and cords, but because it's also the seat most likely to induce nausea as our drivers (usually campaign volunteers) struggled to maneuver our wide-bodied vehicles through city traffic and not lose the first lady's motorcade.

I was sitting next to Tish Durkin, who wrote for the New York Observer. She caught my eye and gestured for me to come closer to hear something. She opened her blue eyes wide, and the hint of a smile played on her lips.

"I'm going to meet you in the swamp tonight," she murmured.

I admit it, I'm kinda slow when it comes to catching on to these antics in the van, so I honestly didn't see the next line coming.

"And if you hear the guns," Tish said, "keep going."

My colleagues were way ahead of me. From the seat in front of us, someone called out, "What if we hear the men?"

Tish called back, "Keep going!"

Now I got it. Duh. From the seat behind us, another voice said, "What if we hear the dogs?"

Everyone joined in on the refrain this time: "Keep going!"

I thought of my biggest obstacles to perseverance on the Hillary trail and called out, "What if we have to go to the bathroom? What if we haven't had lunch?"

"Keep going!" the other reporters shouted back. "Keep going!"

By this time we were all cracking up, pumped up and giddy at our cleverness. This didn't feel like work anymore, it felt like I was back in high school, giggling with my girlfriends in the stairwell.

We settled down in time for the next stop, a somber Episcopal church where a bishop told the worshipers they were about to experience a "visitation" from Hillary Clinton. The atmosphere here was subdued, and Hillary was smart enough to save the "Keep going!" routine for someplace else. Instead, she trotted out another one of my favorite Hillary church shticks, which went something like this: "Someone asked me the other day if I prayed. I said, yes, I do pray. I was fortunate enough to be brought up in a home where the power of prayer was understood. But I have to tell you, if I hadn't prayed before I got to the White House, I would have started after I arrived."

It was a funny line, and even in this buttoned-up place, people laughed.

Part of what made it funny was the surprise of hearing stalwart Hillary admit that times at the White House were rough enough to send her looking heavenward for help. Of course, none of us could ever get her to admit that. I remember when she was interviewed by Charlie Rose in front of a live audience at the 92nd Street Y, she had made one of her usual Pollyanna declarations about how she'd managed to find something good in every single day she spent at the White House.

"What was good about the impeachment?" Rose had asked.

"What was good about it was that we protected and saved the Constitution," she had said without a moment's hesitation, conjuring up a vision in my mind's eye of Hillary, like Dolley Madison saving George Washington's portrait from the fire set by the British, throwing herself in front of the document signed by our first president as Republicans approached.

Now we were on to our third church of the day, St. Luke AME, where the preacher told his congregation, "I'm glad we have a first lady of this country who has held her head high, and who is a scholar, and a lawyer, and a teacher, and a mother, and who is more than capable of being the senator from the state of New York!"

Next up, Hillary. She started with "What a day the Lord has made," thanked everybody for their prayers over the last eight years, and launched into the "Keep going!" routine. But this time, just when I thought it was over, she added a piece I'd never heard before.

"We have to keep going to freedom and opportunity," she said, her voice slowly getting louder. "And I will go to the Senate to continue that fight. I will go to the floor of the Senate every day and work my heart out for you. And I will not turn back! No matter who's behind me! Or what they're saying, or what they're doing!"

By the time she was done with that little speech, she was shouting, the audience was cheering like crazy and I was scribbling in my notebook: "VRWC after HRC again." (That's shorthand for "vast right-wing conspiracy.")

Then she segued back to familiar territory: "Because there is one thing you know about me. When I tell you I'll stick with you... "

I started gathering up my things in preparation to leave, and an older lady sitting behind me taps me on the shoulder. "She's going to be the first woman president," she informed me. "You know that, don't you? Maybe not in my lifetime, but you mark my words, it's gonna happen someday."

I was tempted to say, "There are a lot of Republicans who agree with you," but I held my tongue and thanked her for sharing her thoughts.

The week before, a preacher had made the same prediction. "We're sorry we're losing the president," the Rev. Charles W. Mixon had told his congregation at Maranatha Baptist Church in Queens when the first lady arrived. "I think he'll go down in history as the best president we ever had. I'm not saying this because she's here. I'm saying this because of reality."

He added, "Mrs. Clinton has stood in his corner, and now she's here in our state running for senator. I'm telling you, I think she'll be the first woman president in the United States of America, with the help of me and my God." There was sustained applause, and I was so intrigued by the reverend's endorsement that I called him on the phone the next day. I wasn't sure I understood what all this adulation for the Clintons from the black community was based on. It's not like Bill passed some great civil rights law; if anything, I would have thought welfare reform might have hurt his support among black voters.

Mixon had an interesting take on it. "Clinton has a black secretary," he said, referring to Betty Currie. "That means a lot. No other American president has had a black secretary. Plus the fact you had many people in his cabinet who are people of color. When he had trouble, he called Jesse Jackson. He called Vernon Jordan. He realized he needed people of color to help him through this thing. If I am not loyal to a man like that, who am I loyal to?"

And of course, who can forget Toni Morrison's famous statement that Bill Clinton was "the first black president."

Bill Clinton continued to generate goodwill among black voters even after he left the White House, by renting the penthouse of a Harlem building for his post-presidential office. It was also amazing to me how many of these black pastors actually seemed to know Bill Clinton personally. I had never been to most of the churches Hillary visited, despite years of following candidates around on their vote-getting treks, and I had never even heard of a lot of them, despite having lived in New York my entire life. But it seemed as if in every other church we went to, the pastor got up and talked about meeting the president, or speaking to him, or writing to him, or visiting him in the White House. Black voters often complain about being taken for granted by the Democratic Party, but the Clintons were obviously not guilty of this. One Sunday at Grace Baptist, a church in Mount Vernon in Westchester, not far from Chappaqua, the pastor, W. Franklyn Richardson, something of a bigwig in black Baptist circles, introduced Hillary by recalling a phone conversation he'd recently had with the president.

"I said, 'You're my new neighbor,'" Richardson recalled, referring to the Clintons' Chappaqua home, "and Bill said, 'Yeah, and your old friend.'"

A few Sundays earlier, Hillary had been presented with a wedding anniversary present for herself and the president at an old-fashioned wood-frame church in the Bronx called Emmanuel Baptist.

"Our president, who we love dearly, and the first lady, just celebrated 25 years of marriage," co-pastor Darlene Thomas McGuire told her flock. "We want her to have a token of our love."

Hillary was then handed a big box wrapped in shiny paper, which we later learned contained a silver ice bucket.

Then McGuire, like a lot of pastors, made a show of separating her tax-exempt church from a political endorsement. "I'm not speaking for the church today," she announced. "But as for me and my house, she's the next senator of the United States." Her lyrical phrasing was right out of the Old Testament: "Choose this day whom ye will serve … but as for me and my house, we will serve the Lord," Joshua 24: 15.

We were then treated to the Harriet Tubman tale, followed by prayers and hymns sung by the entire congregation, with Hillary joining in and McGuire leading.

> *I told Satan, get thee behind*
> *I told Satan, get thee behind*
> *Get thee behind*
> *Get thee behind*
> *Victory today is mine!*

But on the second go-round the words changed. McGuire raised her voice above the rest and loudly led with new lyrics until the congregation heard the change and carried on without her. Hillary, I noticed, wasn't singing this version.

> *I told Lazio, get thee behind!*
> *I told Lazio, get thee behind!*
> *Get thee behind!*
> *Get thee behind!*
> *Victory today is mine!*

Of course, for the rest of the day in the van, we sang nothing else—not because we disliked Lazio or thought he was equivalent to Satan, but just because it was so funny. At the Q-and-A later I asked Hillary what she thought of the new lyrics. She paused for a second, then smiled and replied, "I love hymns."

In October, on a three-day upstate tour, Hillary's motorcade got to Auburn, where, as she'd pointed out in all her church speeches, Harriet Tubman's house is located. Finney told everybody on the press bus that Hillary, safely ensconced in her own van, had something to say to them. She connected her cellphone to a microphone and Hillary's familiar voice came through.

"I thought we would all like to see the Harriet Tubman house," she told them. "But we're running short on time to the next event. So we're gonna have to ... keep going!"

The press corps collapsed with laughter. They also got a nifty little memento of the joke: a laminated press credential bearing a picture of a bus, the words "On the Road with Hillary" on the top, and a tiny "Keep Going!" written across the bottom.

CHAPTER 12

The Anti-Hillary

Rick Lazio all but disappeared from the public eye after losing to Hillary. But anyone running against her in the future might take notes on some of the things that did him in. Sure, it was easy for him to raise money from Republicans around the country, just by defining himself as the anti-Hillary. But it wasn't so easy for him to look good when he had to go head-to-head with her. We soon began to refer to "the stature gap" to explain why he didn't know the name of the president of North Korea, while she could talk anybody under the table on the most arcane topics, from the human genome to world affairs. Here's a look at how Lazio's campaign eventually collapsed against the Hillary machine.

• • •

A lot of politicians write long, single-spaced letters when they're asking for money. But Rick Lazio's most famous fundraising appeal was just three sentences long:

"It won't take me six pages to convince you to send me an urgently needed contribution for my United States Senate campaign in New York. It will only take six words: I'm running against Hillary Rodham Clinton."

That letter helped Lazio raise $40 million in just seven months from Clinton-haters all over the country.

But it was more than just a way to mobilize Hillary's foes. Its message in some ways summed up Lazio's candidacy. He was never able to define himself as substantially more than the anti-Hillary, to the point where some voters didn't even know his name. One of the best stories about his obscurity came from Joel Siegel at the Daily News. Joel was walking next to Lazio in the July 4th parade in Ticonderoga when he heard a woman watching the parade go by repeatedly asking, "Where's Lonzo?"

Lazio was marching right in front of her. From then on, the question "Where's Lonzo?" was frequently heard on Hillary's press van.

When Lazio first entered the race, those of us accustomed to Hillary's personal reserve and lack of accessibility, not to mention Giuliani's penchant for insulting any reporter who asked him a question he didn't like, were initially thrilled by Lazio's gregarious, accessible manner. He was about the same age as a lot of us, while Giuliani and Hillary were a decade or so older than most of us in the press corps. Lazio, like Frank Eltman, was a big Allman brothers fan, and his two little girls were about the same age as my oldest son. Liz Moore of Newsday, who lived in the same town as Lazio, had seen him shopping for the kids at Toys "R" Us.

But Hillary couldn't go shopping at normal stores. She'd be mobbed. And she didn't have to move a muscle to get attention in public spaces. Hundreds of people would just immediately surround her. Lazio never had that problem. He had to stride over to people to introduce himself. In fact, that's how he fell on his face 10 days after entering the race. He was zigzagging from side to side to shake hands with people while marching in a Memorial Day parade in Babylon, on Long Island, when he lost his footing, fell and cut his lip so badly that he needed stitches. And on his last day on the campaign trail, he managed to step in dog shit—a hapless end to what was by then a hopeless effort.

From the beginning, there'd been between Lazio and Hillary what came to be known as a "stature gap." Her resume was loaded compared to Lazio's: He was an average guy, not a star, whereas she'd been making headlines ever since she was at Wellesley. She was a student leader in an era when the all-girl campus went from afternoon teas to women's lib, and she was the first student at Wellesley ever to speak at commencement. Her remarks—which included a brash comeback to a Republican senator who'd spoken before she did—made headlines in the Boston Globe and got her picture in Life magazine.

At Yale Law School, she met Bill Clinton and cultivated Marian Wright Edelman, the head of the Children's Defense Fund, as a mentor. From there she went to Washington to help research the constitutional grounds for impeaching Nixon—"the real impeachment," as she likes to call it. Bill talked her into moving to Arkansas with him, and as his political career bloomed with her help, she worked as a law professor and then joined Little Rock's most prominent law firm. She was named to American Lawyer magazine's list of the country's 100 most influential attorneys and was always involved in some commission or other, whether it was chairing a committee on women in the legal profession for the American Bar Association or reforming the Arkansas educational system when she was the governor's wife. In the White House, she simultaneously became one of the most reviled and one of the most admired first ladies ever. Her health care reform effort was a complete debacle, yet for her Senate run she managed to transform that failure into a symbol of perseverance. Her very first speech to New Yorkers on the subject back in the spring of 1999 was the "I come from the school of smaller steps now" approach. But by the end of the campaign, she was no longer talking about health care ideas in a small voice. She was instead roaring sound bites like this: "I believe health care is a right, not a privilege!" and getting ovations in response.

Once in a while, an event in New York would be related to her work on international affairs, including her championing microloans for female entrepreneurs in developing countries, and we'd be thrust into the odd world where Hillary was no longer the candidate struggling to win over undecided suburban women or the subject of some scandal involving Bill's old girlfriends, but was instead a revered international icon, famed as a feminist from Kampala to Berlin.

One of the finest moments in Hillary's career had been a 1995 speech at a conference on women's rights in Beijing. It was a tough critique of abuses of women around the world delivered at a time when the United States was muting its criticism of China's human rights policies.

"It is a violation of human rights when babies are denied food, or drowned or suffocated, simply because they are born girls ... It is a violation of human rights when women are doused with gasoline, and set on fire and burned to death because their dowries are deemed too small," Hillary had declared, adding, "Human rights are women's rights and women's rights are human rights, once and for all." The Chinese government blocked transmission of the speech on radio and TV.

In the middle of the Senate campaign, the United Nations held a follow-up conference to measure progress on women's rights in the five years since the meeting in China. Covering Hillary at this Beijing Plus Five conference in New York gave her Senate correspondents a small window on her international celebrity. I was astounded when women from Malaysia and Benin came up to me and started reciting the details of Hillary's life, saying they couldn't understand why New Yorkers wouldn't want her to be senator when it was perfectly obvious to them that she would be president someday.

We couldn't help but notice that Lazio wasn't being invited to give speeches at the United Nations. Sure, Hillary could say silly things about the Yankees or pander to the Jewish voters with the best of 'em. And in the early days of her campaign, she stepped on every ethnic land mine in the city of New York, made stupid mistakes at Listening Tour events and couldn't generate a sound bite if her life depended on it. But if Hillary started out all substance and no sound bites, by the time Election Day rolled around, she'd figured out how to deliver both. Lazio, in contrast, was too often all sound bites and no substance.

Lazio also had some notable gaffes. In a speech on foreign policy, he referred to the president of North Korea as "Kim Jong the Second" instead of "King Jong Il." It was understandable: The letters I and L look like the Roman numeral II in some typefaces, and Kim Jong was the son of the previous leader. But it was an error nobody could imagine Hillary making.

Another way in which Lazio epitomized the un-Hillary was the makeup of his campaign. He was surrounded by a bunch of white guys just like him. Only two women were on his staff, Eileen Long and Mollie Conkey Fullington, and by the end of the campaign, both of them had been relegated to handling the public schedule for Lazio's wife, Pat, and traveling with her. And Eileen hadn't been just a random hire: She was the daughter of the head of the Conservative Party, Mike Long, who'd endorsed Lazio.

On Hillary's side, not only was the candidate a woman, but the staff was largely female. Sure, Harold Ickes, Bill de Blasio and Howard Wolfson were important players, but there was also Ann Lewis, the senior campaign adviser; Mandy Grunwald, the campaign's media consultant, who created the ads; Neera Tanden, a brilliant young lawyer, the daughter of Indian immigrants, who was Hillary's main policy adviser on the issues and also the deputy campaign manager; Katrina Hajagos, Hillary's personal photographer; Kelly Craighead and Allison Stein, the two blond personal assistants who were never more than a few feet from the first lady's side; June Shih, a young Chinese-American speechwriter, and the two Karens and Cathie Levine, who worked with Howard in the press office.

And finally, there was a difference in the makeup of the press corps. On Lazio's side, the number of women covering him ranged from zero to three. On Hillary's side, there were plenty of women. With the exception of writers for the three big dailies, the Times, the Post and the News, the first lady's press corps included women from Newsday, the AP, the White Plains Journal News, Reuters, ABC, NBC, CBS, WNYC-AM, the Forward, USA Today and various other news organizations that covered her periodically. I went to an all-girls high school, and many a day on the campaign trail, that's what it felt like.

One day when I was covering Lazio, I got my period on the way to catch the press bus, and let's just say I needed to change clothes. Had it been the Clinton van instead of the Lazio bus, I could have told everybody what happened and they would have waited for me. But I didn't have the nerve to describe my problem to the men on the Lazio bus. Fortunately, the press bus was running an hour late. That gave me enough time to scoot into the nearest Strawberry's, buy a $14 skirt with an elastic waistband and change clothes in the ladies room in Grand Central. Had I been returning to the Clinton campaign, one of the girls in the van would have noticed that I was dressed differently, but the boys on the Lazio bus were completely oblivious.

And while kvetching about everything from the lack of food to the lack of access was one of the main activities on the Clinton van, on the Lazio side, Frank told me, "there was this whole macho, bravado thing about who can go on longer without a day off." Gregg Birnbaum of the Post was the winner of that particular contest, counting Yom Kippur as just his only day off in the five months leading up to Election Day. Lazio ended the campaign with 21 straight days on the road, and most of the regular reporters covering him never spent more than a few hours at home during that entire three-week period.

There was also a frat party sensibility on the Lazio bus that all of the Clinton press corps' silly songs and vaudeville riffs on Hillary's speeches just couldn't measure up to. The most notorious prank played by the Lazio reporters came when one of the regular crew decided to take a Sunday off to see the Mets play the Cardinals in the National League championship series at Shea Stadium. Like the others assigned to cover the campaign full time, this person was supposed to be present for every single public appearance Lazio had, just in case of an incident like the lip-splitting fall at the parade, or worse.

"It's a reporter's worst nightmare to be where the story is not," Gregg later pointed out. But this individual decided to take a chance and skip a couple of minor Lazio events upstate to see the game. The events were unlikely to make it into anybody's stories and he figured if any news did happen, his buddies would fill him in.

The other guys spent the day razzing their absent colleague:

"What a dog!" "He really sucks!" "Wouldn't it be cool if something happened to Lazio while he was at the Mets game?"

It wasn't much of a leap from that line of thinking to orchestrating a prank. As the Lazio reporters watched the Mets game on satellite TV aboard the bus at around 9 p.m., Joel Siegel of the Daily News placed a call to their unsuspecting colleague in the stadium. He even disguised his voice, identified himself as someone from the victim's place of employment, and said, in a frantic, pleading tone, "Where are you? We've been trying to get hold of you for a half-hour! There's an AP report that Lazio's bus ran off the road upstate and crashed. There's injuries! Hello? Are you there? This is really big!"

Within seconds, Gregg's cellphone rang. The boys on the bus looked at each other and smiled. It was the panicked victim calling for help.

Gregg answered, "but I was already laughing so hard that all I could manage to say was, 'They're coming out of the emergency room! Talk to Frank!' I tossed my cellphone to Frank because I was about to lose it."

Frank Eltman continued the story, providing details of the phony crash on Route 81 in Syracuse and adding, "It was unbelievable! We crashed into the bus in front of us! We almost died!"

The poor guy on the other end of the line was now freaked out—so freaked out that Frank could barely get his attention when he was ready to fess up. Frank had to call the guy's name a few times before he settled down long enough to hear Frank say, "We're fucking with you! We're fucking with you!" Realizing suddenly that he'd been duped, all the guy could muster in response was an angry, "That's not funny!"

The victim spent the rest of the campaign getting revenge in various ways, like leaving phantom numbers on Frank's beeper so that he would have to chase down calls that hadn't been made.

The following night, the same individual was going to Shea again, this time to actually cover Lazio as he attended one of the games. As they rode an elevator up to their stadium seats with some of Lazio's staff, the congressman filled the few minutes on the elevator by muttering, "Glad everybody's OK from that bus crash." He's been told about the prank by other reporters and a few of his aides.

A week before Election Day in the 2000 Senate race, on a day when I'd already been in the office for 11 hours, I opened what I hoped was the final email of the day, this one from Lazio. I wanted to see my kids that night, so I hoped the email had no news.

The email contained the text of a new radio ad from the Lazio campaign, criticizing Hillary's support for "a radical environmental treaty that would supposedly wipe out thousands of manufacturing jobs in New York." The documentation accompanying the ad identified the treaty as the Kyoto Protocol.

The Kyoto Protocol was widely accepted in environmental circles as a tool to reduce global warming. Lazio always portrayed himself as a big environmentalist; he'd worked in Congress to clean up Long Island Sound and against the strip-mining and coal-burning that result in acid rain damage to forests in the Northeast. It struck me as a little surprising that he'd oppose the Kyoto Protocol. The next day I told Frank Eltman to ask him about the Kyoto Protocol. I explained the context and Frank asked the question. Lazio said he supported "the goals" of the treaty, but not the treaty itself. The protocol calls for reductions in the use of fossil fuels and Lazio said he felt that too many countries like the United States would get stuck with the lion's share of the burdens.

Frank said the other reporters had teased him about asking about something so arcane. But later in the day, as I was whining on the van that there was no story coming out of Hillary's event that day, one of the other reporters said there was a story brewing. The subject: Kyoto Protocol.

Turned out the Clinton campaign accused Lazio of hypocrisy, asserting that he had, in fact, supported the Kyoto Protocol in the past, even though his ad tried to make Hillary look crazy for supporting it. A short time later, the Sierra Club and New York

League of Conservative Voters held a press conference claiming that Lazio had told them that he did support the treaty.

Within hours, Lazio pulled his motorcade over into a highway rest stop in the Bronx to say they were pulling the ad that had led to the Kyoto Protocol debacle.

"Lights out!" Gregg Birnbaum said, summing up the Lazio campaign's collapse. Most voters would never know this ad existed or that it ended up being pulled, but it was a symbol of the larger problems with the campaign.

Not that Hillary wasn't having her own pre-election crisis. It started with an Oct. 25 headline in the Daily News: "Israel Foes Gave Hil 50G." The paper reported that a $50,000 fundraiser for Hillary's campaign held in June in Boston had been sponsored by a group called the American Muslim Alliance. The paper quoted the president of the group as saying that U.N. resolutions permitted Palestinians to "resist by armed force" if peaceful negotiations did not lead to a Palestinian state. The News also printed a photograph of Hillary holding a plaque from the American Muslim Alliance.

Hillary immediately returned the money and said she'd had no idea the Boston event was sponsored by this group. As far as she knew, the Boston event had been sponsored by a Muslim businessman who lived in the area. But if this organization hadn't sponsored the fundraiser, how come they took a picture of her holding this plaque with the words "American Muslim Alliance" printed on it?

"I don't know if any one of you have ever been in this position," she told us at a press conference, "but I have literally been handed thousands of plaques. As I was about to leave, I was handed this plaque. I left. I handed it to an assistant. That is all I knew about it."

Before the Q-and-A was over, we were treated to another installment of "they're all out to get me."

"Fasten your seat belts," she said. "You have no idea what's gonna be thrown at me including the kitchen sink."

The story never completely made sense. The businessman who hosted the event told me that some of the people he had invited to the fundraiser did belong to the AMA, but they hadn't organized it. And later a letter turned up that Hillary had signed thanking the group.

Meanwhile, I learned that the American Muslim Alliance had given money to a number of other politicians around the country in districts with large Muslim populations, and that the organization was considered relatively mainstream by middle-of-the-road members of Congress. The group had even just endorsed George W. Bush for president.

I was disappointed that Hillary had caved so fast without trying to sort out the facts. It felt like she was lumping all Muslims into a category of "terrorists to be avoided." She'd won enormous praise for hosting the first celebration at the White House marking the end of the Muslim holiday Ramadan, but her staff told me there was no way she could make the fundraiser look acceptable, so she dumped all associations with it.

But I was also disappointed with my own inability to sort out what had really happened. In "The Boys on the Bus," Brit Hume complained that his fellow campaign correspondents "claim that they're trying to be objective. They shouldn't try to be objective. They should try to be honest. And they're not being honest. Their so-called objectivity is just a guise for superficiality. They report what one candidate said, then they go and report what the other candidate said with equal credibility. They never get around to finding out if the guy is telling the truth. They just pass the speeches along without trying to confirm the substance of what the candidates were saying. What they pass off as objectivity is just a mindless kind of neutrality."

Crouse added: "A reporter was not allowed to make even the simplest judgments; nor was he expected to verify the candidates' claims ... Using the time honored techniques of objective journalism, they gave equal weight to each man's charges."

If I had one big regret in my coverage of this election, it was the feeling that too often I was guilty of precisely those sins—just relaying the charges from both sides without ever knowing what the truth was. Had Hillary and her staff lied about who sponsored the fundraiser, or was she being unfairly accused of something? The next time I was on the van, I asked my colleagues what they thought. Was the fundraiser sponsored by this Muslim group, or not? A few accepted her explanation, and a few did not. Maybe it was better not to make that judgment after all, but instead just supply what both sides were saying and let the readers decide for themselves.

One improvement in the Internet age in campaign reporting: The web makes it easy to research and fact-check what candidates say in real time. Every debate is now followed by fact-check stories that tell voters whether the candidates are flip-flopping or accusing their opponents of things they've never done.

Writing about the debates between Hillary and Lazio was another situation in which it was difficult for reporters to make a judgment beyond the back-and-forth. In their debate in Buffalo, which proved to be a turning point in the campaign, I thought Lazio did a great job, that he'd finally distinguished himself and taken Hillary on.

But that's not how it came across on TV, and that's not how the voters took it. He was seen as having jumped on Hillary after she'd answered a sensitive question about her marriage. He declared that the upstate economy had already "turned the corner … There's been great progress," while Hillary had connected with upstate voters about the state's dearth of jobs.

And most memorably, Lazio was seen as having tried to bully her by leaving his podium and crossing the stage to confront Hillary about a campaign finance issue, carrying a pledge he wanted her to sign.

"Why don't you sign it?" Lazio said as he thrust the piece of paper in Hillary's face. "Right here, right here! Sign it right now."

I was sitting in a pressroom adjacent to the TV studio where the debate was taking place, watching it on a screen. I'd be lying if I didn't admit that there was something vicariously thrilling about watching Lazio try to pin Hillary down. It was like he was living out my fantasy.

Of course, she didn't sign. She kept on smiling and said she'd be happy to agree to the ban when and if Lazio could produce signed agreements from outside political organizations like the state Conservative Party and the National Republican Jewish Coalition that had been using soft money to pay for TV ads for Lazio.

A few minutes later, I saw on a photo editor's computer screen the picture that the AP photographer had shot of the exchange over the finance issue. It showed Lazio towering over Hillary, his finger in her face, as she physically shrank back from him. It was an unforgettable image, one that would end up on a lot of pages the next day.

An exchange about Hillary's marriage during the debate also played on voters' sympathy for her. It began when one of the questioners, Tim Russert of "Meet the Press," showed a clip from the famous "Today" show interview in which Hillary blamed rumors of Bill's philandering on the "vast right-wing conspiracy."

"Do you regret misleading the American people?" Russert asked her.

She looked pained for a minute, but I didn't feel too sorry for her. I had to assume she'd expected the subject to come up one way or another, and I also knew that anytime Hillary could play the victim and get people to feel sorry for her, it reinforced the notion many voters had that she deserved respect for her poise and bravery in the face of all this humiliation. Her answer, delivered in a humble tone of voice, played to all of that.

"Obviously, I didn't mislead anyone," she said. "I didn't know the truth. And there's a great deal of pain associated with that. And my husband has certainly acknowledged that and made it clear that he did mislead the country, as well as his family."

Now it was Lazio's turn. "Frankly," he said when she was done, "what's so troubling here with respect to what my opponent said is somehow that it only matters what you say when you get caught. And character and trust is about well more than that. And blaming others every time you have responsibility, unfortunately that's become a pattern, I think, for my opponent."

Whew! Rick wasn't going to let a thing like sympathy get in the way of punching her when she was down! I kinda respected him for it. But it turned out that I was out of step. The consensus the next day seemed to be that a bunch of guys had beat up on Hil, and Lazio had joined in when he should have stepped aside.

"I think we in the media have a high tolerance level for harsh rhetoric and political stunts that the average voter might not have," said Gregg Birnbaum of the Post. "We judge it from the perspective of the political theater that we think debates are, but average voters don't look at things the way the media does."

In the days that followed, focus groups and polls showed Lazio taking hits, especially from women. Even those who hadn't seen the debate had seen the photo of Lazio bearing down on this smaller, older woman. The next day, WCBS-TV's Marcia Kramer asked Hillary if she'd wanted to "punch his lights out" during the exchange. And Hillary had answered, "The thing that probably prepared me best to deal with things like that was having two younger brothers." Lazio, in turn, said he knew what it was like to deal with Hillary because he has older sisters. So now the New York Senate race had been reduced to a food fight between an annoying little brother and a bossy older sister.

A few days later, Frank called to dump some quotes from Lazio characterizing the criticism of him as sexist. I actually agreed with Lazio on this one. I think if Hillary had been a man, Lazio wouldn't have seemed like such a cad. Still, as I turned the "this is sexist" quote into the lead of our Senate story, I knew he'd done a foolish thing by saying it.

After all, wasn't it Hillary who should have been complaining that the coverage of her campaign was sexist? All the talk about her clothes and her hair and her marriage, the quotes from the Hillary-haters about her being a doormat, the constant credibility battle she fought to have us and the voters take anything she did as first lady seriously. But I never heard her complain that the coverage of her was sexist.

(What irony it was to watch as polls in her second presidential campaign showed some younger women turning away from her. Hillary the trailblazer, Hillary the groundbreaking feminist, had become the establishment figure next to Vermont Sen. Bernie Sanders, the Democratic Socialist taking on Wall Street. Hillary brought millennial icons like Lena Dunham in to try to woo young women back, and older stateswomen like Gloria Steinem and former Secretary of State Madeleine Albright even scolded the female turncoats. "Just remember, there's a special place in hell for women who don't help each other," Albright said at one event.)

Bill's philandering came up in the 2016 race, too, as Donald Trump called Hillary an "enabler" for staying with him. That was something that Marcia Kramer brought up in a second Lazio debate, asking Hillary, "Why, after all the revelations and pain of the last few years, and because you are such a role model, why (have) you stayed with your husband?"

"For my entire life, I've worked to make sure women had the choices they could make in their own lives that worked for them," Hillary replied. "I made my choices. I'm here with my daughter, of whom I'm very proud. We have a family that means a lot to us ... I can't talk about anybody else's choice. I can only say mine are rooted in my religious faith, in my strong sense of family, and in what I believe is right and important. I want to go to the Senate to stand up for women's choices and women's rights."

This time, Lazio was on his best behavior. "I think that was Mrs. Clinton's choice and I respect whatever choice she makes. The fact is, this race is about the issues, about who can be most effective for New York."

But I couldn't help but think that one important element— love—was missing from the list of reasons Hillary had given for keeping her marriage together. How about just saying, "Hey, I love the guy!" and leave it at that.

The debates also illustrated how silly most of the campaign email was. A minute or two after each debate began, both campaigns would start a mad rush to discredit what the other side was saying. The Clinton campaign emails about Lazio were called "Rick Lazio Reality Checks," while the Lazio emails about Hillary were called "Truth: Lazio Fact Versus Clinton Fiction."

It all made me wistful for the Schumer-D'Amato campaign, when we'd gotten this many emails from either side: zero.

We also got blitzed with emails about the texts of all the silly ads the campaigns were unveiling at the 11th hour, including Lazio ads inexplicably titled "Peach" and "Banana."

"Banana" featured a woman on the phone in her kitchen preparing food and reading a newspaper. The woman is telling the person on the other end of the line, "OK, so Hillary's not a real New Yorker. I've got other concerns. Like my husband and I. We started at the bottom and worked our tushes off. No, but Hillary, she just wants to start at the top, you know, the senator from New York. I mean, why not town council from Chappaqua or something? How about Congress? Sure she's involved with children's issues, but so am I, I've got two kids. No, just because someone is first lady doesn't mean they get to be senator right away. Certainly not a New York senator."

All this drama inspired me to write a TV ad about my own stupid life. I called it "Persimmon." The text went like this:

"For more than 30 years, this woman has been writing about Hillary's Senate campaign. Her 3-year-old tried to stop her, but she kept on typing. Her 7-year-old tried to stop her, but she kept on typing. The kids' pet snake died because she forgot to feed it, but she kept on typing. She's been ordering pizza for dinner for the past 15 months, but she just keeps on typing.

"Now she needs your help to keep child welfare from putting those kids in a home where someone will pay attention to them. Because there's one thing you know about Beth Harpaz. When she tells you she's on deadline, she's on deadline."

Finney once said something to me about how "campaigns are the kinds of experiences that change you in ways that you don't really appreciate at the beginning." If there was one thing I had learned about myself during this campaign, it was that I needed a job that allowed me to be home every night for supper.

I emailed "Persimmon" to Eileen Murphy. Her response was worthy of something Hillary herself might say: "I care deeply about these children."

CHAPTER 13

Senator Clinton

Election night 2000 brought victory for Hillary and the Democrats in New York at the same time that it unleashed anguish for the party nationally. A Supreme Court ruling would eventually give the White House to Republican George Bush. But at least the Dems could savor Hillary's triumph: She'd made history in the Senate race, and she'd trounced her Republican rival. Her impressive 12-point margin of victory—bigger than anyone had anticipated— gave me pause to reflect on what her campaign had been all about: connecting with women and overcoming the public's and the media's perceptions about who Hillary Clinton is and what she stands for.

• • •

Election night, Nov. 7, 2000. It was almost 11 p.m. when Rick Lazio finally took the stage at the Roosevelt Hotel in Manhattan to state the obvious. Standing in front of an American flag, he grinned that boyish smile that made him seem so likable and came up with a nice made-in-New-York metaphor about the World Series to describe his defeat to a woman who claimed to love the Yankees.

"I feel like the Mets," he said, referring to the team's World Series loss to the Yanks that year. "We came in second."

Then he mentioned that he'd just called Hillary to congratulate her, and everybody in the room started booing. So what if she won big time? That didn't mean Republicans had to like her.

The last words of his concession speech were barely out of his mouth when every newscast in New York switched to Hillary's headquarters, a few blocks away at the Grand Hyatt. Columns of red, white and blue balloons festooned the ballroom, and a giant "Hillary" banner was draped on the stage. Four hundred journalists were among the 2,000 people waiting for her to arrive. But in a sign of what was to come in the weeks ahead, people were already obsessing about the presidential race, watching the results on big-screen TVs.

Finally, Hillary appeared on the ballroom stage, Bill and Chelsea by her side, with Moynihan and Schumer joining them. Hillary had chosen, for this night, a turquoise pantsuit, the better to stand out among the dark suits in her entourage, and a brighter, snazzier look than her usual workaday black. As the crowd cheered and chanted "Hill-a-ry!" the president "guided Chelsea into buffer position between them," recalled my colleague Tom Hays, who covered the event for the AP while I spent the evening in the office analyzing exit polls. "It was not unlike the scene of the family heading off for vacation after Bill finally fessed up to the Monica thing, where the three were holding hands, Chelsea in the middle, walking across the White House lawn to a waiting helicopter."

Schumer delivered the "she did it the old-fashioned way—she earned it" line that he'd been using for the past week, and Moynihan mumbled a few words by way of introduction. But there would be no tribute from the president tonight; there could only be one Clinton in the spotlight this time.

"Wow!" said Hillary, as she surveyed her adoring fans and paused to savor the moment she'd begun imagining back at the height of the impeachment scandal. "This is amazing!" And in some ways it was. A first lady had made history. And a carpetbagger with a suitcase full of scandals had outdone a squeaky-clean local boy.

But the news of her victory was not just that she had won, but that she had won by such a large margin. Even her staff had anticipated no more than a 4- or 5-point win. Instead, she beat Lazio by 12 points. It was a rebuke not just to Hillary-haters who'd paid so much money to see her lose, but to anyone who ever said she wouldn't succeed and shouldn't try. The numbers from her win also proved that women were her most loyal constituency: She won 60 percent of all female voters, 65 percent of working women, 75 percent of New York City women and 55 percent of upstate women. The votes from upstate, the most conservative part of New York's electorate, were particularly impressive for a Democrat.

I thought back to the early months of the campaign—the jokes about the Listening Tour and her love for the Yankees, the house-hunting that ended in Chappaqua, the split between New Yorkers who shouted "Go back to Arkansas!" and those who swooned and squealed at the mere sight of a first lady in their midst.

I tried to remember why, back in early 1999, I had been so reluctant to believe she was going to go through with it. At the time it had seemed impossible that a woman who'd never held elective office and never lived in New York would attempt this audacious feat, especially with all the baggage of her marriage and the impeachment. But even though it had seemed ridiculous back then, now, looking back from election night, it seemed almost inevitable.

In fact, Hillary's win did feel strangely anticlimactic, as if it were a logical outcome to anyone who'd been paying even a little attention. Sure, Hillary started out the campaign by pissing off Jews, gays, Puerto Ricans and nearly everybody else in New York, but she ended up an expert on everything from treating asthma in the Bronx to getting high-speed Internet access in Buffalo. Lazio, in contrast, fell down and split his lip on his way into the race and stepped in dog shit on his way out. In between, he'd stuck his finger in Hillary's face, called the leader of North Korea "Kim Jong the Second," and earned not one but two insulting nicknames—Lonzo and Little Ricky—from a press corps that had no particular reason to love Hillary, her Secret Service agents and their German shepherds. There was only one learning curve in the campaign and it was all hers.

"We started this great effort on a sunny July morning in Pindars Corners on Pat and Liz Moynihan's beautiful farm," Hillary said as a lead-in to what would be the most-quoted line from her acceptance speech. "And 62 counties, 16 months, three debates, two opponents, and six black pantsuits later, because of you, we are here."

To those who voted for her, she added a "thank you for opening up your minds and your hearts, for seeing the possibility of what we could do together for our children and for our future, here in this state and in this nation." To those who voted against her, she pledged "to work in the Senate for you and all New Yorkers ... to reach across party lines to bring progress for all of New York's families. Today we voted as Democrats and Republicans; tomorrow we begin again as New Yorkers."

She was gracious in recognizing the man she was replacing, saying, "Sen. Moynihan, on behalf of New York and America, thank you," but oddly subdued in acknowledging the man who had played a much bigger role in her transition from political spouse to political spotlight, a man who, like Moynihan, was leaving public office after decades—Bill Clinton. Only after thanking Chuck Schumer, Rudy Giuliani, Rick Lazio, every Democratic official in the state of New York, her mother and her brothers, did she thank "my husband and my daughter." Chelsea had that doll-like smile plastered on her face while Bill looked on like Pygmalion, smug yet proud. Beneath a shower of confetti, Hil kissed and hugged sundry and assorted Dems like Nita Lowey and Carl McCall. No public hug took place between Bill and Hil. It seemed odd that they didn't want the cameras to record one, but the moment when it would have made sense for them to embrace quickly passed and was swallowed up in the chaotic celebration around them.

Then, together, the Clintons stepped down from the stage and waded into the crowd to greet their fans, their arms extended to shake the outstretched hands. For a moment, the president's eyes teared up, and as he left the ballroom, he told supporters, "I'm so proud of her."

When I left the office that night a little after 3 a.m., Hillary had long since vanished as a topic of discussion on TV, and Bush had been declared the winner of the presidential race. But by the time a taxi delivered me to my door a half-hour later, Bush was no longer the winner and the country had embarked on the strangest post-election season of my lifetime. All I kept thinking was, "Thank God this didn't happen in the Senate race!" I was ready to go back to living a normal life. I had been counting on the Wednesday after the election as a day without Hillary for a long, long time and I pitied my counterparts in Washington and Florida who would not be doing their laundry or going on vacation or sleeping late as so many of them had planned.

I went to bed around 4:30 a.m. Wednesday morning and woke up at 9 a.m. It was the most restful, dream-free and longest period of uninterrupted sleep I'd had in days. When I finally got to the office, I spent the rest of the day taking down all the cartoons, clippings and photographs of Lazio and Hillary that had appeared on my desk, on the wall behind my chair and on the office bulletin boards over the past two years, including life-size masks I'd made of each of their faces from photographs. Then I dragged six cartons of campaign financial reports out from under my desk and left them by the garbage. Last but not least, I filled up two more cardboard boxes with dozens of videotapes of campaign ads.

Later that day, Hillary held her victory news conference in Manhattan, thanking "the members of the press, particularly the hearty band who covered me from July of 1999 until last night." She was then asked if next time she'd run for president.

"No," she said without hesitation. "I'm going to serve my six years as junior senator from New York." She kept her promise on the six years, and even won re-election for a second term in the Senate in 2006 before announcing what both her supporters and her enemies had seen all along as the next step: a run for president in 2008.

Although she introduced a record 70 bills as a freshman senator, she kept a relatively low profile during her first year in office. Perhaps she was heeding the words of Republican Trent Lott, who said within a day of her winning, "When this Hillary gets to the Senate—if she does, maybe lightning will strike and she won't—she will be one of a hundred and we won't let her forget it."

Ironically, by the time her swearing-in rolled around on Jan. 3, with the president sitting with Chelsea in the spectators' gallery, Lott and another of the old-line Republicans, 98-year-old Strom Thurmond, appeared to have softened their public stances a little. Thurmond rose to greet her just after she'd taken the oath of office, asked, "Can I hug you?" and wrapped her in a bear hug. Lott later said, "Well, she certainly is going to get extra attention because, she is, after all, the first lady, the first one ever to be in the Senate."

One aspect of Hillary's victory that got lost in the history and novelty of a first lady getting elected was that she became the first woman ever to hold statewide office in New York in her own right. (We'd had female lieutenant governors before, but they don't get their own line on the ballot—they're part of the governor's ticket.) Before Hillary was elected, New York had never had a woman in any of the four statewide elected offices—governor, state attorney general, state comptroller or U.S. senator. Geraldine Ferraro, one of the most famous female politicians in the country for her historic 1984 vice-presidential run, hadn't even managed to win the state Democratic primary in the 1998 Senate race. Her loss in that campaign to Schumer, who was much less well-known, inspired Hillary-skeptics to draw comparisons. So what, she's a feminist icon. So what, she's a celebrity. So what, she has name recognition. If Gerry couldn't do it, an Italian Catholic from Queens, then Hillary the Midwestern WASP couldn't do it either.

But a friend and colleague of mine at the AP, Karen Matthews, observed that maybe it took a woman from out of state, a carpetbagger, to persuade both upstaters and downstaters that she was worthy of support. And who better to be all things to all people than Hillary, who could be sophisticated and Ivy League on the Upper East Side of Manhattan in her black pantsuit, but then go upstate, play up her Midwestern accent, and be introduced by a local politician—as she was on one of her early trips to Buffalo—as someone who "shares our values" because she grew up in a Great Lakes state.

"I did grow up on the Great Lakes!" she crowed in response,

and it occurred to me that I'd never heard her use that line in the Bronx or Queens. But it sure went over big in a city dominated by Lake Erie to have the first lady remind everyone that she had grown up near Lake Michigan.

Although I only accompanied Hillary upstate a handful of times, each time I went I also couldn't help but be struck by how well she fit in there. I was used to seeing her as the only white lady in a black church, or the only WASP at a luncheon of Jewish and Italian ladies. I'll never forget watching her in that crowd in Buffalo where she used the Great Lakes line. I looked around at the swarm of people and realized that unlike any group she'd ever spoken to in New York City, this one looked just like her! All these women had hair the color of straw, big blue eyes, round noses and cheeks like rosy pancakes.

"I got a beauty shop and I got a lot of ladies who want to work for her," the proprietor of Williamsville Hair Fashions told me as I canvassed the crowd for comments. "These ladies range from 25 to 75. She's hitting all kinds of women in different stations of life, because she's for families and children."

Giuliani was still in the race at the time, and another lady grabbed my arm and started telling me why he didn't stand a chance in Buffalo. "He's from the city, and they think anything north of there is another country," she declared. "He thinks fighting crime and drugs and this and that is important, but it doesn't have anything to do with us. He's as much of a foreigner as anyone else. If he's gonna go to the Senate and only represent New York City, I don't need him! She's here to represent the interests of New York state."

When the election results came in, it was clear that Hillary's twin strategies of trying to win over women and paying a lot of attention to the upstate economy had paid off even more than her staff had anticipated. Months before the election, John Zogby, the Utica-based pollster, had told me Hillary was smart to spend so much time in upstate regions perceived as conservative.

"Upstaters have usually felt as if they were orphans," he said. "What's actually been important to upstate voters is physical presence. This candidate actually came here, spent some time here. And not just at the end. We can go back to the beginning, to the Listening Tour. It was criticized by a lot of people for a lot of reasons. But she was there. She physically touched down in every one of 62 counties."

On the Friday after Election Day, Hillary went on a victory tour to thank her supporters upstate. After all the no-news days everyone had put in on the road with Hillary before the election, nobody expected to get a decent story this fly-around. Especially with the drama over the presidential vote just beginning to unfold, Hillary's victory suddenly seemed almost uneventful. But she managed to make news that day in a way we weren't used to: on purpose. Without any warning to her staff or the press, she got up in front of her supporters upstate in one city after another and called for the abolition of the electoral college. She'd been senator-elect for all of three days, and here she was already leading the charge to rewrite the Constitution.

In fact, even in her remaining days as first lady, hardly a day went by without some sort of Hillary story in the news. First there was her new book about the history of the White House, then there was yet another trip to Ireland, not to mention the controversial $8 million book deal for her memoirs and the purchase of a 5,500-square-foot Washington mansion for $2.7 million, a nice pied-a-terre for the Clintons away from the Chappaqua home. Even her committee assignments sparked interest: the Health, Education, Labor, and Pensions Committee, which gave her a platform to continue her advocacy for health care reform and better schools; the Environment and Public Works committee, which Moynihan had served on; and the Budget Committee, which drafts Congress' annual budget plan.

Hillary had also scheduled a first lady trip to Vietnam for right after the election, but somehow I hadn't realized the president was going, too. When I saw a headline in the paper that read, "Clinton Visits Vietnam," I assumed it was about Hillary. I started reading the story only to discover that Hillary barely merited a mention; this article was about Bill visiting Vietnam. So why didn't the headline say "Clintons" visit Vietnam?

Then I remembered. When Hillary's alone, she's the news. When Hillary was with Bill, he was the news, and she's only the first lady. A first lady doesn't count for much, even after winning a Senate race. What really mattered was that the president of the United States was on a friendly mission to our former enemy.

In a photograph from Vietnam, Hillary was pictured walking behind Bill. In accounts of events where he spoke, she was reported to have said ... nothing. It reminded me of something she once said when asked why all this work she was claiming to have done as first lady, on issues ranging from cancer to child welfare, had gone unnoticed.

"When you come out of the White House, there really is one voice, and that's exactly as it should be," she'd said. "Everybody is there because of the president. He selects the vice president, he brings his team with him, everybody there is furthering the president's agenda, so that no matter how much you do to help create positive results for the people as part of that overall agenda, it's only appropriate that the American public doesn't know much about it, because that's not where the rightful attention is drawn."

Hillary's side trips in Vietnam without Bill did get some coverage of their own, I guess because at those events she was free to speak and be heard without worrying about whether she was turning his solo act into a duet. She took a field trip to see microcredit in action in a small village. She attended a conference on the exalted role of Vietnamese women in their culture. But the story in The New York Times quoted an expert saying, "For all the talk about the advanced status of women, the numbers just aren't there." The expert pointed out that while more than a quarter of Vietnam's National Assembly are women, "in the more influential Politburo, there is only one woman out of 19 members," or just over 5 percent.

Those percentages sounded awfully familiar to me. I pulled out my "Almanac of American Politics 2000" and started flipping through the pages, counting women's faces. Out of 50 governors, three were women; that's 6 percent. Out of 100 senators, nine were women; once joined by Hillary and the new female senators from Washington state, Michigan and Missouri, women comprised 13 percent of the Senate. The percentage of women in the House was only slightly larger. In America, as in Vietnam, for all the talk about the equality of women, our numbers weren't there either. (Those numbers had improved by 2015, when women made up about 20 percent in the U.S. Senate and House of Representatives.)

I then started reading the biographies of the six women in New York's 31-member congressional delegation. All but one was older than Hillary. Their life stories included Louise Slaughter, first elected to public office at age 47, after her children were grown; Nita Lowey, whose resume included being a PTA mom in Queens before she was elected at age 51; Sue Kelly, first elected at age 58 after she had raised her family in the Hudson Valley district she represented, an area where she'd been a volunteer and had her own business renovating buildings; and Carolyn McCarthy, a nurse who ran for Congress at age 52 to work for gun control after her husband was murdered and her son wounded by a gunman on the Long Island Rail Road.

In some respects, Hillary's life story was similar: She was first elected to office at age 53, as her daughter prepared to graduate from college and her husband prepared to leave the White House. But what was really stark was the contrast between all these women with their late-in-life transitions into politics and the many men who were elected as 20- and 30-somethings. Chuck Schumer, fresh out of law school at the tender age of 24 when he took elective office for the first time, as a state assemblyman from Brooklyn. Anthony Weiner, who took over Schumer's congressional district in Brooklyn, just 27 when he was first elected to the City Council, and 34 when he went to Congress. Rick Lazio, 31 when he entered the Suffolk County legislature, and 34 when he went to Washington.

"I think the rhythms of our lives are different from men's," Diane Chapman Walsh, the president of Wellesley College, told me back when rumors first surfaced that Hillary might run for office and I just didn't understand why she would embark on a new career like this so late in her life. "We can stop and take stock and wonder about something quite different after our children have grown up and our lives are changing in various ways. That isn't as true for men."

Even though women ended up voting heavily for Hillary, back when Giuliani was still in the race, polls showed white women preferred him over Hillary. I wanted to do a story exploring why, and Frank Eltman suggested that I go interview some soccer moms, a demographic group that had gone big for Bill Clinton. So one Sunday in early spring, just as the soccer fields in Westchester were turning green, I headed up there and spent the day chatting with women in jogging suits as they cheered their daughters' teams.

It turned out to be all about credibility. The feeling was that Hillary just hadn't paid her dues.

"We have some very good Democratic politicians who could have been the candidate for Senate, but it was given to her," complained one woman.

"She's smart and very focused, but I don't think she's right for it," said another woman.

"She's the president's wife, but that doesn't give her a right to run," said a third.

Around that same time, I noticed a change in Hillary's exit routine. For months, when she was done speaking somewhere, she'd magically disappear behind a curtain or a stage and then zoom away in the Speedwagon. It was good way to avoid reporters, and it probably made the Secret Service happy as a secure, fast way to move her from one controlled environment to another. But as spring wore on, Hillary began spending more and more time hanging out after events, shaking hands and taking a minute to chat with people. At restaurants and hotels, she'd meet everyone who wanted a word with her, then made sure to also say hello to the cooks and the waitresses. At outdoor events, she'd sign autographs and pose for pictures with her fans, then go around and thank every police officer on security detail. Once, as she walked down a street in Queens, I heard her call over into the back of a churning truck, "Thank you for the job you do every day!"

Hillary's meet-and-greet efforts were particularly intense at ladies' lunches, especially those where the invitees included suburban women with ambivalent feelings. A lot of these luncheons were themed around a good cause like cancer research or child abuse prevention, and the audiences tended to be politically diverse, as opposed to a union rally or Democratic fundraiser filled with Hillary supporters. So that made the events interesting for the press corps, because we could get before-and-after quotes from these undecided voters. Did their opinion of Hillary change once they'd heard her speak or got to shake her hand?

You betcha. "I'm not undecided anymore," they'd almost always say as they saw me coming back to find out what they'd thought of her speech. Inevitably they made the same three observations. One, she's so much prettier in person than she is on TV. Two, she's so much nicer and warmer than they thought she would be. And three, she's so brilliant, how could you not vote for her? It seemed that only die-hard Republicans couldn't be convinced to support her after hearing a good rendition of her stump speech and seeing her willingness to hang around afterward to meet every woman who lined up for a hello.

I also started hearing rumors that her campaign was holding meetings for women who didn't like her. The meetings were hosted by women who knew her and could speak favorably about her. I even came across a couple of women who'd attended some of these meetings, but they'd all been asked not to speak to the press and they took that pledge seriously. Eventually, near the end of the campaign, when the polls finally began to show Hillary leading Lazio among white women, Ann Lewis, who had worked as a top adviser to the president before becoming one of Hillary's senior campaign strategists, told me what these meetings were all about.

"The idea of women getting together in their homes to talk about things that matter to them really is a tradition if you think about it," she said. "We called them advocates' meetings. They were led by women who really knew her, women who could say, 'I've known her, I've worked with her, she's somebody who rolls up her sleeves and works.'"

Ann also defined Hillary's problem with women and explained the campaign's line of attack in solving it: "Women responded to how hard she has worked over the last year and a half. Talking to women on the way in with her, there were questions about whether she was serious about this, whether she was going to work to earn it. I think her opponents had painted this as a 'she thinks she's entitled.'... But she proved her credibility. She committed to it. She always expected she would have to work hard to get it."

About a month before the election I interviewed a woman, Sheila Gordon, who'd hosted one of these advocates' meetings in her apartment. "I'd invited mostly people in my neighborhood who I knew had reservations about Hillary," she said. "But I think that virtually every woman I had invited, who came feeling on the fence and unhappy about Hillary, feels confident voting for her now."

What accounted for the change? "The length of the campaign has allowed people to disengage themselves," she said. "It is so challenging to see ourselves out there. And we see a lot of ourselves in her—like the question of why we didn't do things more quickly" in terms of fulfilling long-held dreams or advancing careers.

I thought back to what Diane Chapman Walsh had said, about the rhythms of our lives being different from men's. Sheila was on the same wavelength.

Hillary, she added, is a "lightning rod for all kinds of things. We really haven't learned to evaluate a woman who's accomplished, and feminine, and also like us." She said she thought it took time for women voters to say, "If her marriage works out differently than mine, I still would like to have a good, strong, smart person as my senator.... Some people want her to show all her emotions and start crying every time someone brings up Monica. To a certain extent, people want to know that it hurt her a lot. But we are holding her to a higher moral standard."

One of the women I'd met at a Hillary event in September, a

teacher who'd started out the afternoon describing herself as an undecided voter, ended up telling me she'd vote for Hillary. "A year ago I would say, 'I don't know why she stayed with him,'" meaning Bill. "But I'm not even thinking in that area anymore," she told me.

I also called some of the soccer moms back in the fall, five months after I'd interviewed them. "She earned my respect, she's earned my vote," one of them told me. "It's her understanding of the issues, her passion for the issues, her ability to listen."

"She really has proven herself," said another one. "I've changed my mind about her. I like a lot of her stands on the issues. I know she's an advocate for children, even if she doesn't have children in the local schools." In other words, it's OK to be a carpetbagger if you can prove you know what you're doing.

The Clinton campaign staff always felt the press corps underreported how much support for Hillary there was all along. "There could be 200 people at an event cheering for her and one person with a 'Go Home' sign, and the 'Go Home' sign will always make it into everybody's story," campaign aides would commonly grouse. And I think it was true, as another reporter once put it to me, that a lot of us were "uncomfortable in conveying the positive reactions Hillary was getting."

But when you've heard 100 gushy tributes to a woman who says she's been handed "thousands of plaques," you don't really feel that it's news, in the strictest sense. Tish Durkin of the New York Observer once pointed out the "Miss America quality" to much of Hillary's support. She was always being given bouquets and baskets and compliments about her appearance. It was hard to predict whether that type of adulation would translate into broad political support. And when someone who strives to be as perfect and scripted as Hillary does make a mistake or gets heckled, that's the definition of news, and therefore worthy of a story.

Besides, the people who hate her are always more dramatic than the people who love her. One weekend in Ithaca, as Hillary and Chelsea arrived for a rally at Cornell University, a man began screaming, well within earshot of the first daughter, "Who's your father raping now?" A month after the election, a Syracuse man was arrested for threatening Hillary's life in a letter sent to the house in Chappaqua. And then there was the Slap Hillary website, where you could interrupt an image of the first lady babbling with a click of your mouse and watch her get smacked into silence.

Some Hillary supporters complained that the press dutifully reported on the racism that Barack Obama faced in the 2008 election, but ignored the misogynistic attacks on Hillary. Looking back, I have to say we largely ignored that aspect of the 2000 race as well. And yet we were well aware that the hatred of Hillary was a potentially serious matter. We covered Lazio at every public appearance in case he had another pratfall, but we all knew the real reason we had to stay in the room until Hillary left or wait outside until she was safely in her van. We almost never talked about it, but it was always there in the back of our minds: the possibility that, someday, someone might try to hurt her.

Still, I wonder: Did I pay too much attention to the Hillary-hater who ran down the street screaming "You're an enabler" and not enough to the women who told me how brilliant she was? Would the coverage have had a different tone had the pre-election polls indicated more strongly how decisive her victory would be? All along, we depicted Hillary as someone who was attempting to scale a different mountain with Lazio nipping at her heels, instead of depicting her as someone who actually had a lot of built-in advantages: her celebrity, her marriage to a president New Yorkers strongly supported, the fact that Democrats outnumber Republicans 5 to 3 in New York, and her name appearing on the ballot beneath that of the 2000 Democratic presidential nominee Gore, who won New York by a landslide even though he didn't end up in the White House. If you looked at the campaign with those factors in mind, the race was hers to lose instead of a challenge for her to win. In the end, the percentage of New Yorkers who supported Lazio on Election Day was nearly identical to the percentage who had supported him the weekend he entered the race. The Republicans probably could have run anyone on that ballot and done nearly as well. Those people who screamed "Go back to Arkansas!" weren't part of a growing movement; they were a static minority.

On the other hand, while they could tell she was being received well upstate, even Hillary's staff never took victory for granted. "Everyone who says Lazio ran a terrible campaign, and everyone who says they knew he was going to lose all along, did not live the life we led," one of her top advisers told me after she was sworn in.

The focus on scandal and screw-ups flared again shortly after the Clintons left the White House, reviving the dynamic we so often experienced during the campaign of the press corps running after bad news, while Hillary just kept plugging away on her favorite unglamorous issues. She followed through on her pledge to introduce legislation to help the upstate economy; she held a news conference to express her opposition to the new attorney general, John Ashcroft; she even shlepped to a couple of black churches, pledging to make racial profiling illegal and expressing support for a new holiday honoring—guess who!— Harriet Tubman!

But all that boring good news about New York's junior senator was drowned in a flood of headlines over Bill Clinton's pardons and their connections to Hillary. The pardon recipients included Marc Rich, whose ex-wife Denise was a frequent White House guest and prominent supporter of Democratic Party causes, including Hillary's campaign and Bill's Arkansas library. Four Hasidic men whose sentences were commuted came from New Square, one of the only Hasidic communities to support Hillary for Senate. And Hillary's brothers, Tony and Hugh, successfully sought pardons for several felons who'd made their acquaintance. Hugh even took— but was forced to return—a $400,000 fee for his pardon-getting services. (If I'd still been on the campaign van, a parody of the "Chattanooga Choo-Choo" would have been a natural: "Pardon me, Hil, I need a presidential pardon!")

The uproar over the pardons even overshadowed the scandal over the thousands of dollars in gifts the Clintons received, as if they were newlyweds, when they permanently left the White House for Chappaqua—china, televisions and furniture, including (oops!) a few items that were supposed to have been left in the White House and not removed for the Clintons' personal use. Of course, Clinton defenders pointed out that these gifts and even the pardons were not all that different from the patterns set by previous presidents. But as I always tell my kids, just because somebody else uses a bad word or acts up, doesn't mean it's OK for you to do it.

In the middle of the pardon furor, I called a few of the soccer moms again, and they told me they felt betrayed. They'd supported Hillary because she seemed so competent, but with all the new scandals, they were reminded of their initial reservations about her candidacy. A Marist poll taken near the end of February 2001 showed that about 60 percent of New Yorkers believed Hillary had done something unethical or illegal in connection with the pardons, but the survey, like other recent polls, also found a bedrock of support that roughly equaled the percentage of people who voted for her, with a little over half of those polled saying they still thought she'd be a good senator.

And that, it seemed to me, was the story of Hil's political life, just as it was for Bill's. She'd get dragged down again and again by scandals, some real, some exaggerated or imagined by her enemies, some that were really more her husband's fault than her own. And then eventually, simply because she'd show up to work each day and plug away on issues like the upstate economy, health care, education and racial tolerance, she'd win everybody over again. If all it took to wipe Hillary out was a string of bad headlines, she'd have been finished off by the Suha kiss, the St. Pat's parade, the FALN flap, and every other controversy from the early days of her Senate race. Instead, just like her husband, she always managed to stage a comeback.

During the first few months of the Bush administration, it was hard to remember that the Clinton administration was over. After all, Bill and Hil were in the news every day; George and Laura were all but invisible. One reporter for a tabloid told me that with Republicans in the White House, the governor's mansion and City Hall, the Clintons were the only available target. It reminded me of something Crouse had written in "The Boys on the Bus": "Conservative Republican presidential candidates usually receive gentler treatment from the press than do liberal Democrats. Since more reporters are moderate or liberal Democrats themselves, they try to offset their natural biases by going out of their way to be fair to conservatives ... Reporters sense a social barrier between themselves and most conservative candidates; their relations are formal and meticulously polite. But reporters tend to loosen up around liberal candidates and campaign staffs; since they share the same ideology, they can joke with the staffers, even needle them, without being branded the 'enemy.' If a reporter has been trained in the traditional, 'objective' school of journalism, the ideological and social closeness to the candidate and staff makes him feel guilty; he begins to compensate personally, the harder he judges him professionally... Most of the reporters who covered George McGovern in the fall campaign preferred him to Richard Nixon and ended up voting for him (if they voted at all)."

Were we harder on Hillary because we were trying to compensate for some built-in pro-liberal bias, or because we identified more closely with her than with Lazio? I can honestly say that I'm not sure whether the average reporter's politics were closer to Hillary's or Lazio's. A lot of reporters I know voted for third-party candidates in the last few elections ranging from Ross Perot to Ralph Nader. And the general public might be surprised to hear that we actually didn't talk much about our personal politics during the campaign. It's not like we ever sat around on the van debating the death penalty or late-term abortion or gun registration. We just tried to get the quotes right and complained about the lack of news, not to mention the lack of food.

Many of the reporters I know also have a self-imposed policy of not voting in elections they cover. Myself, I don't have a hard-and-fast rule on it, but I did fall victim to a different occupational disease: cynicism. In the end I couldn't bring myself to vote for anyone in the Senate race.

But regardless of whom they voted for or whether they voted

at all, I'm not sure how many reporters could say of the Clinton campaign, the way Crouse did of the McGovern campaign, that they personally "preferred" Hillary to Lazio. Often, covering Hillary was like running through an obstacle course, only to find when you finally got to the candidate, there was no there there. And if what Crouse referred to as "social barriers" existed in the New York Senate race, they were not between the press and Lazio, they were between the press and the Democratic candidate, simply by virtue of her first lady trappings and her reserved personality. That's why it was such a big deal anytime she did drop the formalities and crack a joke with us, invite us for coffee or hand out doughnuts.

The morning she turned 53, for example, she greeted voters in Grand Central, then turned to us for a press conference. We sang her "Happy Birthday," and I handed her a little cupcake with a candle on it. We'd actually had a debate among ourselves about whether it was "over the line" to give Hillary a cupcake, but, hey, sometimes you just throw all caution to the wind. Then someone asked her, "Do you get to do anything fun today at all?"

A huge smile broke across her face as she spread out her arms as if to embrace the entire press corps.

"Well, here I am with all of you!" she said, her voice dripping with sarcasm as we started laughing nervously. "It's the way to start any day! And now I have to show my absolute affection and devotion to my hardworking press corps that has followed me through—how many counties? Sixty-two! And what is it that we have in common? … Thank you, Bob!" (Here she nodded to Bob Hardt, who had called out the answer she was seeking.) "The human genome! We are 99.9 percent the same. I find it absolutely thrilling that you and I are 99.9 percent the same!"

She then handed out doughnuts to each and every one of us. It was about as startling as the "C'mon, let's go have coffee!" day when we ended up chatting about potty-training, or the day she sent a basket of candy back to the press van or handed out the cookies with her picture on them. On the other hand, as Maggie Haberman of the Post pointed out to me once, it was also a little unsettling that anytime Hillary had an informal interaction with us, she made it clear that she knew exactly what we were saying behind her back—thanks to the campaign staffers who reported back to her all the little things we made fun of in the van.

"It was funny, like, OK, she's mocking herself and that's kind of cool," Maggie said. "She was connecting with us and attempting to humanize herself. But she also knows what we're saying when we're not in her presence. On one level, 'Yes, I'm connecting,' but on another level it's like, 'Don't think I don't know what's going on.' It's like your mother."

I'll never forget how, on Lazio's first weekend on the trail after launching his campaign, the baby-faced congressman from Long Island wrapped his tongue around the white ball of a vanilla ice cream cone at the Byrne Dairy in Syracuse while photographers snapped away. It was not a pretty picture, but it was an interesting picture, and for a guy as little known as he was at that point, running against a woman as famous as Hillary, it was a smart thing for him to do. The picture was widely used, it made his face a little more familiar to voters around the state and it made him look like a regular guy—the type of grown-up who licked a drippy cone with the enthusiasm of a little kid. It was also a stark contrast to the day in June 1999 when we weren't allowed back inside the Tavern on the Green until Hillary had finished eating lunch.

But a year later, she understood the value of chowing down in public. Two months before the election, Hillary and Bill visited the state fair in Syracuse. As cameras recorded the big moment, she tore into a messy sausage sandwich with gusto, her mouth wide open as the thing spewed stuffing out the sides. The president dabbed her mouth with a napkin.

Once she lost her first lady staff and started her new job as senator, she even let her glued-down coiffure give way to the occasional bad hair day. The Washington Post described this new, less-than-flattering look as her hair hanging "like rain-battered weeds." Asked about it at a press conference, Hillary simply said that some days she had time to fix it, and some days she didn't.

My mother, a lifelong Republican, worked, as a young woman, for Sen. Margaret Chase Smith, the Maine Republican who was the first woman to serve in both houses of Congress and the first to serve four full terms in the Senate. Margaret Chase Smith was also the first woman—long before Elizabeth Dole—to try for the presidency on a major party line. "Is a woman acceptable?" she wrote to my mother late in 1963 as she mulled over her decision. She eventually ran against Barry Goldwater in several primaries, and her name was submitted for the nomination at the 1964 Republican convention. I grew up hearing the story of how, in 1950, Margaret Chase Smith became the first member of the Senate to stand up to Sen. Joseph McCarthy, who was leading a witch hunt for Communists.

"I don't want to see the Republican Party ride to political victory on the four horsemen of calumny—fear, ignorance, bigotry and smear," she'd said. Other families hung pictures of the pope or John F. Kennedy in the hallway, but in my house there hung a framed photograph of Margaret Chase Smith, not in homage to an early feminist, or to a great Republican, but just because she was a decent, courageous individual who stood for the right things, and who had some small connection to the life of our family. That she was a pioneering woman in politics really had nothing to do with it.

But I wonder sometimes what she would have thought of Hillary. I'm sure she would have disagreed with a lot of her politics, spoken out about the Clinton scandals, and been privately appalled by some of her personal choices, but I bet there might also have been some mutual admiration had she and Hillary been contemporaries. I certainly can't imagine Margaret Chase Smith using the phrase "maybe lightning will strike" in the same sentence as the first lady's name. And I suspect they could have had an interesting conversation on the subject raised in the letter to my mother: "Is a woman acceptable?"

When I asked some of the other women who covered Hillary to share with me some of the moments that stood out to them on the campaign trail, many of them talked about gender and the historic nature of what she'd done. But they also said how hard it was to feel like they'd connected with Hillary as a real person.

Noreen O'Donnell, who covered the Senate race for The Journal News, a Gannett paper in suburban Westchester, said she never understood why Hillary was such a "lightning rod. She doesn't seem radical enough to me to be the lightning rod. ... She's talking about women's issues, yet she followed a sort of traditional woman's life—she got married, went to her husband's home state, worked her career around his. I don't think most women live either a perfect feminist life or a conventional life. It's a hodgepodge of different things."

She also understood why Hillary kept the press corps at arm's length, even on that memorable day when she invited us for coffee: "She genuinely was trying to reach out to people and have a relaxed time. But you know she's also thinking, 'Even though I see these people every day, they are not my friends. I can buy these people coffee today and try to have a relaxed moment with them, and if I screw up tomorrow, they'll be all over me.'"

Tish Durkin, who covered the campaign for the New York Observer, said Hillary's "aversion to self-revelation" was understandable, given her history. But "there is a difference between questions that are insulting and constitute garbage-picking through the soul of a human being, and questions which are either very material to one's fitness for office or kind of interesting on a human level and harmless." She remembered asking Hillary one day what was an example of something someone had written about her that she felt wasn't true. "She could have said some issue or 'I think I'm softer' or 'I never thought my hairstyle would become so big,'" Tish said. "I mean, it's not a trick question. But she said something like, 'I really can't speculate on other people's motives.' If there was ever a time for someone to open up slightly, that was it. And I just felt sorry for her in a way."

Ellen Wulfhorst, of Reuters, said Hillary was "not very likable. She's very, very distant. She's in one room, her emotions are in another. I understand why she would be so guarded. She was the most humiliated woman in the world. ... I wish I liked her more. Then I'd think, maybe it's even sexist to even think that; would we ask that of a male candidate?"

Lauren Burke, a photographer who'd covered politicians like John McCain, George Bush and Al Gore before she covered Hillary, said she gave Hillary a lot of credit for the fact that there were so many women working on her campaign. Covering politics, she said, "one of the things you find is that there are always a lot of male people running around with clipboards. I thought it was really impressive that Hillary Clinton had a lot of young female people running around doing the work."

Eileen Murphy, who covered the campaign for ABC News, said that looking back, all she could think was how normal the campaign had been, despite all the build-up, the coverage and the fear that something dramatic was going to unfold. The reality was, "there seemed to be days and days where nothing happened." She recalled the day when Chelsea was asked to say a few words at an event in Queens, but all she said was hello: "That was like a metaphor for the whole campaign. You get all worked up and then she just says hello."

As for me, I'll never forget a Hillary rally that Bill Clinton attended about three weeks before the election. Everyone was shouting to him, not her, and when it was over, a sea of arms reached up from the audience to touch him. He walked to the edge of the stage, leaned over and stretched his arms down into the crowd. It was like watching Elvis. He seemed to get his lifeblood from the adulation. An agent on either side grabbed him to keep him from falling in or being pulled in. It was so different from all the ladies' lunches where Hillary was shaking hands politely on one side of a velvet rope.

I had one last chance to see Bill and Hillary in action before the Clintons left the White House. A couple of weeks after the election, I got invited to a White House Christmas party. The party was just for journalists, and it was on a Sunday evening. At first I wasn't going to go. I just kept saying, "I'm not going to let Hillary mess up another one of my weekends! I'm not shlepping all the way down to

Washington to spend another hour with her!" But then everybody told me I'd be crazy not to go. So finally I called to RSVP and of course they asked for my date of birth, Social Security number, photo ID—all the usual hassles of covering Hillary.

There were hundreds of people there when we arrived. Most were people who usually cover the White House. But there were some Hillary regulars. We were all trying to get to a long table laid out with shrimp and little quiches and sushi, and you had to jostle your way in. It was actually kind of humiliating, like trying to score the last doughnut in a box on the press van.

But I was surprised at how beautiful the White House was and how awesome it felt to be there. The walls were covered with portraits of all the presidents and first ladies, and there were Christmas decorations everywhere: giant wreaths and a gingerbread house and a couple of big trees all twinkly and lit up. I walked into a small, peaceful room named for Ben Franklin, and for a while I just looked out the window at the white columns outside and thought to myself how strange it was to be on the inside looking out instead of on the outside looking in.

Finally we headed downstairs for a photo and handshake with Bill and Hillary. All these hundreds of people were funneling into a single-file line. It took more than an hour, but eventually it was our turn. Someone announced our names, and there we were with the Clintons. Up until that moment, I'd always thought of Bill as the people person, the one who loved human contact. But the funny thing about going to the White House was that they were the opposite of what I'd expected. The president acted like a robot and Hillary was the charming one.

I guess Bill probably hates the press to begin with, and it must be awful to stand for three hours at a party shaking hands with all these people you don't know and don't like. He just kept saying over and over in this monotone, "Thank you very much. Thank you very much." His face was completely expressionless and his eyes were narrowed down to tiny little slits. I tried to say something like, "Hi, I'm Beth Harpaz, I covered Mrs. Clinton's Senate campaign in New

York," but all he said in response was, "Thank you very much, thank you very much."

Hillary was standing next to him, wearing this red plaid outfit that was very Christmas and very un-Manhattan. She put out her hand and said, "Hi, Beth!" in a big, warm tone of voice. I hadn't seen her since the election, so I congratulated her and said what I thought was appropriate for a journalist to say, something about how hard she'd worked, and how much she'd impressed us all with her energy.

Then I introduced my husband, assuming she'd never remember the brief moment in the church on the Lower East Side at the housing forum where he showed up with the kids.

As she shook his hand, a look of recognition flickered on her face. "I think we met before, didn't we?" she said.

I was amazed at her memory. She really had turned into the consummate politician. "Um, actually, that's right, you did," I mumbled.

My husband smiled. "Beth would never say this," he told her, "but we're thrilled that you won."

I shot him a look and nearly kicked him. I mean, what's with the "we"?

Hillary smoothed it over in an instant. "Well, now we've got to get to work on housing all those other issues, right?" she said, raising her eyebrows meaningfully. We laughed and nodded, but I was stunned that she'd recalled the connection to the housing forum.

Our little moment with the Clintons was over; it was time for us to move along. As we stepped away through a doorway, I noticed Howard Wolfson standing there. I was just about to make a joke— had he been posted there to spin the Christmas party in a positive way, or did he just happen to be there as we walked by?—when I heard Hillary speaking again in my direction.

I turned back to catch what she was saying.

"Say hi to the kids," she called after us, "will you?"

"I will," I called back. "I will."

ABOVE: Rep. Rick Lazio, R-N.Y. demands that first lady Hillary Rodham Clinton sign a pledge banning so-called "soft" money from her campaign during the first debate in their race for the U.S. Senate in Buffalo, N.Y., Sept. 13, 2000. (AP Photo/Richard Drew)

LEFT: Senate candidates Lazio and Clinton listen to a question during their second debate in New York, Oct. 8, 2000. (AP Photo/Richard Drew)

BELOW: Democratic presidential hopeful, Sen. Hillary Rodham Clinton, D-N.Y., greets supporters at a Rally for Change at the University of Iowa, Iowa City, July 3, 2007. (AP Photo/M.Spencer Green)

Supporters of Democratic preside hopeful Sen. Hillary Rodham Clinton, D-N.Y., cheer befor Democratic preside debate in Las Vegas, 15, 2008. (AP Phot Ronda Churchill)

Democratic presidential hopefuls Clinton, D-N.Y. and Sen. Barack Obama, D-Ill., participate in a Democratic presidential debate in Myrtle Beach, S.C., Jan. 21, 2008. (AP Photo/Mary Ann Chastain)

Democratic preside candidate Hillary Rodham Clinton sp in Council Bluffs, Iowa, Oct. 7, 2015. Photo/Nati Harnik

ABOVE: Clinton speaks as Sen. Bernie Sanders of Vermont looks on during the CNN Democratic presidential debate in Las Vegas, Oct. 13, 2015. (AP Photo/John Locher)

LEFT: Hillary Clinton laughs during a commercial break at a Democratic presidential primary debate in Des Moines, Iowa, Nov. 14, 2015. (AP Photo/Charlie Neibergall)

BELOW: Bernie Sanders listens as Clinton speaks on screens in the media filing center during a Democratic presidential primary debate at Saint Anselm College in Manchester, N.H, Dec. 19, 2015. (AP Photo/Michael Dwyer)

Bob Kunst, of Miami Beach Fl, wears a Hillary Clinton mask as he stands outside the North Charleston Coliseum, in S.C. Jan. 13, 2016 (AP Photo/Rainier Ehrhardt)

RIGHT: Hillary Clinton speaks at the NBC/YouTube Democratic presidential debate at the Gaillard Center, in Charleston, S.C., Jan. 17, 2016 (AP Photo/Mic Smith)

BELOW: Hillary Clinton takes a selfie with a supporter after speaking at Valley Southwoods Freshman High School in West Des Moines, Iowa, Jan. 24, 2016. (AP Photo/Patrick Semansky)

AFTERWORD

Looking Back, Looking Ahead

As I revisited the text for this new edition, I was struck over and over by how many of the issues that came up in the 2000 campaign are still being debated by Hillary Clinton and her opponents and remain foremost in the minds of voters. Peace in the Middle East is even less imaginable now than it was then. The controversy over the shooting of an unarmed black man, Amadou Diallo, by police in New York City was as big a story then as similar shootings around the country are now. The school shooting at Columbine in Colorado was fresh on voters' minds in 2000, and the debate on gun rights was making headlines too. Hillary even participated in a protest in Washington against gun violence called the Million Mom March. Environmental concerns were a factor in the 2000 campaign as well: One of the last dust-ups in the Senate race concerned an ad about the Kyoto Protocol, an international agreement to reduce global warming. The 9/11 terror attacks had yet to occur when Hillary ran for Senate, but the World Trade Center had been bombed in 1993, and the USS Cole was attacked by al-Qaida suicide bombers off the coast of Yemen just a month before the 2000 election. Quality affordable child care, the cost of college tuition and health care were also issues that were part of Hillary's agenda then as now. And my own experience as a working mother covering a campaign in which there were more women reporters and campaign workers than other races I'd written about also has echoes today, as was described in a recent POLITICO article called "The Women in the Van," about the vast numbers of female reporters assigned to cover Hillary's 2016 campaign.

But I don't want to suggest that this book is more than a snapshot in time. Despite some of the themes from 2000 remaining relevant, the 2016 campaign has and will have its own dynamics. And we all know that anything can happen in an election. Politicians who look like they're sitting on top of the world can be undone in an instant by scandals or their own words. One unforgettable ad from a candidate or an opponent can have more impact than months of shaking hands with voters. And voters' opinions can change rapidly in response to something said in a debate or even a single photo that shows a candidate behaving in some unseemly way.

Events can also influence voters' perceptions and even alter election logistics in ways that can't be predicted—witness the hanging chads on Florida's 2000 presidential ballots that were said to have confused some voters and helped give the White House to George W. Bush instead of Al Gore. Another example: The 9/11 attacks on the World Trade Center led to the postponement of New York City's mayoral primary, which gave Michael Bloomberg time to build a campaign for mayor that might not otherwise have succeeded.

So it would be pointless, in advance of the 2016 election, to predict who will be the next president of the United States. Social scientists look at changing demographics in the U.S.—more minorities, younger voters, more women, more immigrants—and conclude that Democrats have a built-in advantage in national elections because their progressive platforms appeal more broadly to those voters. Other analysts look at world events, especially the growing fear of terrorism at home and abroad, along with the conservative movement that's given Republicans control of the Senate and the House, and conclude that a Republican candidate could win the White House.

Whether Hillary Clinton succeeds in her quest to become the next president, her campaign and her career will go down in history as groundbreaking for women. I hope that in some small way, "Candidate Hillary" will have contributed to how the story of her evolution from first lady to a politician in her own right is remembered.

—Beth J. Harpaz, 2016

Acknowledgments

Special thanks to Sarah Nordgren, Peter Costanzo, David T. Scott, Lisa Lerer, Paul Colford, Lauren Easton, Hal Hilliard, Sara Frazier, Tina Fineberg and the entire team at Diversion Books for their hard work on publishing the 2016 edition. And to all those who helped with the original edition, thank you, especially the ones whose help consisted of random things like babysitting.

BETH J. HARPAZ covered Hillary Clinton's first Senate campaign for The Associated Press in 2000. She now works as AP's travel editor and is the author of two other books, "Finding Annie Farrell" and "13 is the New 18."

Printed in the USA
CPSIA information can be obtained
at www.ICGtesting.com
JSHW031705140824
68134JS00036B/3516